Cambridge Elements

Elements in the History and Politics of Fascism
edited by
Federico Finchelstein
The New School for Social Research
António Costa Pinto
University of Lisbon

INTELLECTUAL POST-FASCISM?

The Conservative Revolution, Traditionalism and the Challenge to Liberal Democracy

Alberto Spektorowski
Tel Aviv University

Shaftesbury Road, Cambridge CB2 8EA, United Kingdom

One Liberty Plaza, 20th Floor, New York, NY 10006, USA

477 Williamstown Road, Port Melbourne, VIC 3207, Australia

314–321, 3rd Floor, Plot 3, Splendor Forum, Jasola District Centre, New Delhi – 110025, India

103 Penang Road, #05–06/07, Visioncrest Commercial, Singapore 238467

Cambridge University Press is part of Cambridge University Press & Assessment, a department of the University of Cambridge.

We share the University's mission to contribute to society through the pursuit of education, learning and research at the highest international levels of excellence.

www.cambridge.org
Information on this title: www.cambridge.org/9781009533195

DOI: 10.1017/9781009533218

© Alberto Spektorowski 2025

This publication is in copyright. Subject to statutory exception and to the provisions of relevant collective licensing agreements, no reproduction of any part may take place without the written permission of Cambridge University Press & Assessment.

When citing this work, please include a reference to the DOI 10.1017/9781009533218

First published 2025

A catalogue record for this publication is available from the British Library

ISBN 978-1-009-53319-5 Hardback
ISBN 978-1-009-53318-8 Paperback
ISSN 2977-0416 (online)
ISSN 2977-0408 (print)

Cambridge University Press & Assessment has no responsibility for the persistence or accuracy of URLs for external or third-party internet websites referred to in this publication and does not guarantee that any content on such websites is, or will remain, accurate or appropriate.

For EU product safety concerns, contact us at Calle de José Abascal, 56, 1°, 28003 Madrid, Spain, or email eugpsr@cambridge.org

Intellectual Post-fascism?

The Conservative Revolution, Traditionalism and the Challenge to Liberal Democracy

Elements in the History and Politics of Fascism

DOI: 10.1017/9781009533218
First published online: June 2025

Alberto Spektorowski
Tel Aviv University
Author for correspondence: Alberto Spektorowski, albertos@tau.ac.il

Abstract: Is the world facing creeping fascism? And if so, how is it configured in contemporary circumstances? A wide-ranging debate has developed in recent years among scholars increasingly worried by the weakness of liberal democracy and the growing electoral power of national populist movements in Europe. In this account, the rise of the current wave of populism was preceded and is now accompanied by an important theoretical elaboration, initiated in the 1970s in France by the intellectuals of the Nouvelle Droite and continued by Russian, American and Latin American intellectuals and political strategists. The theoretical goal of this metapolitical elaboration is a reformulation of the values of cultural diversity, identity politics and postcolonialism, a process that in this Element is defined as the attempt to decolonize the "postcolonial Western mind."

Keywords: fascism, conservatism, revolution, postcolonialism, traditionalism

© Alberto Spektorowski 2025

ISBNs: 9781009533195 (HB), 9781009533188 (PB), 9781009533218 (OC)
ISSNs: 2977-0416 (online), 2977-0408 (print)

Contents

1 Introduction: Fascism's Resurgence and the Erosion of the Hegemony of Pluralist Liberal Democracy ... 1

2 It Is Identity, Stupid! From the Politics of Rage to Ideological Construction ... 5

3 The French Nouvelle Droite. Between the Conservative Revolution and Traditionalism: Post-fascism and Anti-colonialism ... 21

4 Conclusions: Fascism in the Making? From Metapolitics to Political Praxis ... 61

References ... 67

1 Introduction: Fascism's Resurgence and the Erosion of the Hegemony of Pluralist Liberal Democracy

Is the world facing creeping fascism? And if so, how is it configured in contemporary circumstances?

In recent years, a broad debate has emerged among scholars increasingly concerned by the vulnerabilities of liberal democracy and the rising electoral power of national populist movements across Europe. Today, following Donald Trump's landslide victory in the 2024 American elections, this question is more pressing than ever, leading several scholars not only to voice concerns about the future of democracy but also to revisit the old, seemingly settled debate over what fascism is and how it might reemerge in the modern era.

Among those who advocate for the use of the controversial term *fascism* to describe current developments, some focus on the period of ideological incubation that preceded fascism's rise as a political movement. Historically, this was an era marked not only by intense political polarization but also by intellectual fervor. It involved a dual process: the delegitimization of Enlightenment values and the political ideologies rooted in them, alongside the intellectual construction of a revolutionary "third way" that formed the foundation of fascist and National Socialist ideologies. Through the lens of those dramatic times, this Element explores whether the new values challenging contemporary liberal hegemony have roots in the ideological construction of old fascism. This question is of profound relevance.

At first glance, the defeat of fascism in 1945 also implied the deconstruction of its ideological and intellectual sphere or at least its imprisonment at the fringes of the political debate. This, however, has dramatically changed. In our account, the rise of the current wave of populism was preceded and is now accompanied by an important theoretical elaboration, originally initiated by the intellectuals of the Nouvelle Droite in the 1970s in France and expanded nowadays by a wide variety of intellectuals and communication channels. The importance of this ideological uprising goes well beyond specific electoral turnouts. Indeed, we claim that liberal democracy and its progressive political turn is challenged by much more than a reactionary Trump-style politics devoid of intellectual basis. After three decades of dominance, liberalism is losing its hold on Western minds and it is being attacked first at the intellectual level before being dismantled at the political level. As Matthew Rose (2021) has astutely pointed out, the notion that principles such as human equality, minority rights, religious toleration or cultural pluralism could be outright rejected is bewildering to many.

Confronting the sociology of populism requires one type of struggle, while a metapolitical strategy aimed at undermining the conceptual framework of liberal society demands a distinctly different approach. This is precisely the reality unfolding in contemporary times. This prompts an inquiry into the political tenets of what could be defined as a contemporary conservative revolution and the figures spearheading this ideological development.

The theoretical counterintuitive argument advanced in this Element is that the current rebellion against liberal democracy is scarcely associated with vulgar populist nationalism, white supremacy and Western cultural colonialism. Against all odds, the New Right, serving as the ideological vanguard of what could be defined as a "fascist resistance," is reformulating the idea of identity politics and even postcolonialism, transforming them into intellectual tools of exclusion rather than inclusion. This novel perspective, outlined in this Element, aims to decolonize the "postcolonial Western mindset." It posits that Western original identities should be recognized alongside the "selected group" affected by liberal colonialism (Hull, 2022, 151).

In essence, this argument posits that the legacy of Western colonialism extends beyond the non-Western world, encompassing Europe's Indigenous populations and marginalized groups in America, often labeled "white trash." These groups too are framed as victims of Western liberal colonialism and the Enlightenment's ideals. This Element proposes that this fresh perspective signals a crucial shift toward what could be termed a *new political theory of the Right*. Unlike twentieth-century fascism, which was defined by supremacist and imperialist ambitions, this emerging form of "post-fascist resistance" is largely anti-imperialist and, in many respects, nonsupremacist. It focuses on countering globalist influences, reclaiming national sovereignty from supranational entities and resisting perceived foreign cultural and economic encroachments.

This emerging resistance movement is not solely a rejection of the liberal present but an ambitious, forward-looking project envisioning a new world order centered on the revival of tradition, popular sovereignty and a fresh concept of emancipation. Instead of promoting a hierarchy of nations, this new movement frames itself as a defense of local traditions, distinct identities and self-determination, aligning national resistance with an anti-colonial ethos and reconfiguring the concept of sovereignty in opposition to liberal globalism. This "old-new" utopia not only redefines domestic and international ideals but does so in ways that unexpectedly challenge various political camps. For left-leaning progressives, the postcolonial Right's vision presents a significant challenge by highlighting the paradoxes in identity politics, which may, at times, foster exclusion more than inclusion. Meanwhile, for radical right-wing parties, this new vision could provoke a critical reevaluation of narrow, uniform nationalist aims.

In this way, the postcolonial Right appears to be forging a unique ideological space that defies easy categorization within traditional left or right paradigms.

I suggest thus that the postcolonial Right is crafting a distinct ideological space, one that resists simplistic alignment with traditional left or right orthodoxies and aims instead to upend the established liberal framework entirely. The critical question, then, is how this ideological framework is being constructed and to what extent it is rooted in original fascism.

This emerging trend indeed draws intellectual inspiration from the intersections of the national revolutionary ideology springing from the Weimar conservative revolution of the 1930s, and of the Traditionalism ideological school advocated by esoteric thinkers such as René Guénon and spiritual racists like Julius Evola. At first glance, the intersection of Traditionalism and the Weimar conservative revolution may appear surreal. After all, there seems to be little common ground between the Weimar conservative revolution, which laid the foundations for the fascist "third way to modernization," and the Traditionalist movement, which rejects modernity.

Indeed, unlike the futuristic aspects of fascism, Traditionalism embraces a belief in a revered past and in religious principles. Traditionalism believes in an original millennial and perennial religious tradition that spreads out in different directions, such as Hinduism, mystical strands of Judaism, Christianity and Islamism. However, the Traditionalist turn shares with the conservative revolution a desire for a new postliberal order. What is more important, the fusion between the two currents bridges the gap between traditional identities of the non-European Global South and revitalized Western identities, countering the forces of liberal globalization. To explore how this Traditionalist perspective, together with the values of the conservative revolution, set the ground for a new postcolonial fascism of resistance, this Element will focus on the ideological tensions and encounters of four key political and philosophical figures: the French New Right thinker Alain de Benoist, the Russian philosopher and nationalist right-wing activist Aleksandr Dugin, the political strategist Steve Bannon and the Brazilian intellectual and influencer Olavo de Carvalho. While we recognize that the intellectual current represented by these figures encompasses a broader array of thinkers and activists worldwide, we will focus on these four individuals – who integrate ideological and political activity – as a starting point for understanding this ideological trend.

The Element begins by defining the socioeconomic and cultural conditions that enable a challenge not only to the sociopolitical hegemony of liberalism but also to its ideological and intellectual dominance. It then articulates the political thought of four public intellectuals, portraying them as heirs to the old conservative revolution that preceded fascism. Finally, it examines whether this ideological development could give rise to a common project worthy of consideration.

Alain de Benoist, as the intellectual founder of the Nouvelle Droite, has indeed been a pivotal figure for the European New Right, particularly in promoting an exclusionist identitarianism that stands in contrast to liberal multiculturalism. His vision of a "Europe of its peoples" advocates for a Europe built upon distinct ethnic and regional identities, rejecting the homogenizing forces of liberal globalism. De Benoist's goal is to preserve these Indigenous European identities, believing that such an ethno-regional Europe would liberate the continent from the ideological colonization of Western liberalism, which he sees as a force of cultural erasure. The following discussion in this Element will explore the tensions and intersections between de Benoist's ethno-regionalist framework and Aleksandr Dugin's fourth political theory and Eurasianism.

As is well known, Aleksandr Dugin is a leading figure in Russian nationalism and has exerted a great influence on Russian political thought, particularly in regard to geopolitics and Russia's role in the world. Dugin has advocated for a Eurasianist vision that envisions Russia as a central player in a multipolar world order, counterbalancing the influence of the United States and the West. The question we shall address concerns the compatibility between de Benoist's "Europe of the Peoples" and Aleksandr Dugin's concept of Eurasia. While both thinkers critique liberalism and globalism, they diverge in their solutions. De Benoist's emphasis on preserving the plurality of European identities contrasts with Dugin's geopolitical vision of a unified Eurasian bloc, which transcends national borders in favor of a civilizational unity led by Russia. We emphasize, however, that both concepts serve to reshape the notion of national sovereignty, transitioning it from the framework of the nation-state to that of an ethnically and spiritually defined anti-liberal empire.

Following de Benoist and Dugin comes the figure of the American political strategist Steve Bannon, whose relationship with Trump made of him not only a man of ideas but also of action, at least for a brief period of time. Like de Benoist and Aleksandr Dugin, Bannon is positioned as a Traditionalist figure who critiques what he sees as the encroachments of liberal globalism and the "woke" culture that accompanies it. His advocacy for a conservative revolution in America is rooted in a desire to either restore or preserve what he identifies as the fundamental traditional values of American society. Moreover, by identifying the emerging populist currents worldwide, he has become one of the precursors of a new international populist movement, which, though initially met with skepticism, is now an ideological development worthy of close attention.

Finally, there is the figure of Olavo de Carvalho, a far-right Brazilian pundit and self-proclaimed philosopher who became the political guru of President Jair Bolsonaro by warning of a globalist plot to spread communism and socialism across the world. He was considered by Bannon himself as one of the great conservative intellectuals in the world.

The four characters we analyze share a common belief that we live in an era of turmoil and confrontation with an evil, secular and globalist status quo. The four consider that we are in times of definitions, and the four consider that the only way to recover an ideal, spiritual and orderly society like the one that supposedly existed in the past is through the destruction of today's existing society and its institutions, which will ultimately lead to a cultural and ethnic renaissance. The four of them thus promote traditional values, cultural heritage and anti-wokism as essential components of a counternarrative to liberal globalization. Indeed, they are intellectual revolutionary warriors signaling an end to liberal colonialist culture, an end to political and ideological correctness and, at the international level, an end to unipolarity.

Alongside exploring the convergences among these figures, a central aim of this Element is to dismantle the portrayal of the Traditionalist conservative Right as a monolithic entity. We argue that the theoretical tensions within this movement reveal the depth of ongoing intellectual debates among conservative thinkers – an essential point. The key point of divergence, as we shall see, lies in how each thinker defines the forces of materialism and spirituality, as well as their strategies for overcoming the materialist threat (Teitelbaum, 2020, 2021).

Finally the question remains: How concerned should liberals be about this ideological shift? Indeed, anxieties have grown among liberals as these ideas increasingly challenge the theoretical foundations of liberalism established after the Second World War. European liberal leaders, in particular, have shaped their political outlook and commitment to human rights under the shadow of the Holocaust. By contrast, leaders from the Global South, such as Xi Jinping in China, prioritize their nations' colonial experiences over issues like anti-Semitism and the Western human rights framework. This perspective, shared by numerous developing countries and an expanding segment of Western society, is commonly associated with the *decolonial Left*.

The innovation of this Element, however, lies in tracing the intellectual roots of what we define as the postcolonial Right, which rejects nostalgia for an era marked by the liberal West's dominance in setting global norms and standards. In multiple ways, it positions Xi, Putin and even Trump along a similar trajectory – as direct or indirect critics not only of the liberal world order but also of the foundational ideas that shaped it. In more senses than one, this fascism of resistance envisions the end of the West as we knew it, after the Second World War and the Cold War.

2 It Is Identity, Stupid! From the Politics of Rage to Ideological Construction

After the end of the Communist world, a liberal democratic consensus became the new undisputed normality. Under the new intellectual and ideological regime, human and minority rights were at the forefront of moral and political debate, and the conviction that the power of the majority should be controlled became the norm.

In order to preserve this new normative world, European political leaders followed a complementary strategy to achieve economic prosperity while relegating popular endorsement of policies to the future. As Jan Müller (2011, 128) has remarked, their approach reflected a liberal distrust of democracy; demands for popular and national sovereignty have been widely blamed by political elites for the catastrophes of the first half of the twentieth century. In this zeitgeist, the discussion of ideas was dominated by liberalism whose strategic question was how to make the values of liberal democracy more effective and more inclusive. Some have pointed out that this triumphal liberalism was accompanied by a new post-materialist agenda that has brought about a greater emphasis on freedom of expression, environmental protection, gender equality and the inclusion of gay people, handicapped people with disabilites and people from other cultures and countries and foreigners (Inglehart, 1971). Multiculturalist, postmodernist and post-materialist ideas gave expression to this new spirit, which during the 1990s gained institutional expression. The new understanding was that the historical nation-state in Europe was over and that a liberal European communitarian identity had become hegemonic (Risse and Grabowski, 2008, 9–11). However, despite the optimism, Ronald Inglehart has been trenchant in stressing the problematic transformation of liberalism in a so-called post-materialist society. On the one hand, the adoption of a post-materialist agenda has been fruitful in boosting liberal values and tolerance. On the other, it has opened the door to a backlash that has brought about a "retrogression toward authoritarian and xenophobic societies" (Ingelhart and Welzel, 2005, 4; Ingelhart and Norris, 2017). While Inglehart represents those who hope that what they regard as a populist retrogression is a short-term deviation from a developmental trajectory to which modern societies will eventually return, scholars like Ingolfur Bluhdorn and Felix Butzlaff are less optimistic. In reality, there is no way back to the traditional liberal, democratic, inclusive, egalitarian debate. In the current shift from classical liberal modernization to a "second-order emancipation," established concepts no longer serve to define what is happening at the sociopolitical level. It is not only the idea of liberal modernization and reform liberalism that is losing traction under the weight of neoliberalism. The Marxist view of corporate capitalism's support for an authoritarian state to fight an organized working class also now seems irrelevant. In modern neoliberalism, Silicon Valley entrepreneurs, for example, would stand in favor of an open and global economy, enjoying the declining power of labor unions while at the same time supporting minority rights and "woke culture" (referring to all struggles against racism and a pro-immigration and multiculturalist stance). Moreover, movements like Occupy Wall Street, though driven by economic grievances, were fundamentally rooted in a predominantly college-graduate, white-collar demographic – one that contrasts sharply with the traditional working class found in postindustrial or rural areas. This distinction underscores a broader divide within the Left, where the focus on identity and social issues has sometimes overshadowed class-based advocacy for economically disadvantaged nationals. The intersection of "woke" culture and international institutions with this absence of a pro-working-class Left has created fertile ground for the convergence of populism and a conservative intellectual revolution (Clarkson, 2004). From a somehow similar perspective, Beth Rabinovitz suggests that the new economies of speed and scale created by the Industrial and Digital Revolutions, accompanied by economic crisis, mass migrations and terrorism, turned democratic nations inward (Rabinovitz, 2023). This is indeed the battleground especially for right-wing populist movements.

An ongoing debate regards the essence and ideological features of this right-wing national populism. What would be the differences between a right-wing populism and fascism, if any? For several scholars, populism is a parasite on liberal democracy, one that grows in times of crisis to ultimately endanger its host. For others, populism represents an illiberal democratic attack on an undemocratic liberalism, a movement devoid of a thick ideology, which can also be defined as a political style (Mudde, 2004; Muffit, 2016; Müller, 2016; Urbinati, 2019). Scholars like Ernesto Laclau argue that populism is a way to construct the political. It articulates heterogeneous unsatisfied demands, thereby creating an original discursive formation and a new "collective will" (Laclau, 2005). An ensuing question, however, is whether this "collective will" could survive without being associated with nationalism. Current examples of left populism such as Syriza in Greece, Podemos in Spain and the Five Star Movement in Italy might exemplify a type of left-wing populism whose association with nationalism was punctual tactical associations rather than genuine political articulations. Christopher Bickerton and Carlo Invernizzi Acetti made a great contribution to the understanding of these two populist movements by shifting the attention to the synthesis between populism and technocracy. Even though appeals to the popular will and to competence are often rhetorically deployed against each other, the authors claim that both concepts advance an unmediated conception of the common good. Both populists and technocrats advance either a monolithic conception of the "popular will" or the specific conception of political "truth" to which technocrats claim to have access. Both populists and technocrats hate professional politicians (Bickerton and Invernizzi Acetti, 2021).

The question, however, is whether that is enough for political survival. As Daniel Rueda (2020, 51) adds, hegemony is achieved thanks to a nationalist stance that serves as a bonding agent for several heterogeneous demands. The national factor thus is the main political actor. It is therefore clear that populist leaders would always recur to the myth of the nation in order to construct the "people" as against foreign interests. This seems to be an instinctive act of populist leaders in order to trigger popular rage to the pains produced by socioeconomic modernization associated with foreign and local elites. In national populism, then, the nation acts as the key empty signifier and the people, the nation and the leader appear to take an almost theological value. The problem, as Andrew Arato (2013, 167) argues, is that putting "a human actor like 'the class' or 'the people' or 'the leader' in the place formerly occupied by theological or religious categories like 'God' or 'Christ' or 'pope,' means ... to attribute to them supernatural traits that the empirical referent cannot sustain." This can only lead to a deadly authoritarian suppression. For some scholars, political activists and journalists, these developments in contemporary politics may warrant the use of the term *fascism* to describe them. President Joseph Biden recently described the Republican Party as dangerously consumed with antidemocratic forces that had turned toward "semifascism." It is not just Trump that is the problem; it is the entire philosophy that underpins the Trump phenomenon (Viser, 2022). Defeating fascism, in a broad sense, means overcoming a governance model that prioritizes security, uniformity, conformity and social validation for the dominant majority at the expense of civic freedoms, legal accountability, independent media, diversity and minority rights (Tisdall, 2024). Despite the seeming distance of such practices from the Western democratic paradigm, an increasing number of observers argue that we are witnessing a resurgence. That spirit of alert has led scholars such as Federico Finchelstein to claim that populism today emerges as a post-fascism that reformulates fascism for democratic times. In the cases of Trump and Bolsonaro, Finchelstein would define them as not totally but "wannabe fascists" (Finchelstein, 2019, 2022; Homans, 2024). Enzo Traverso (2019) uses the concept of post-fascism precisely to define this hybrid phenomenon. Neither the reproduction of old fascism nor something completely different can define the wide variety of heterogeneous and transitional movements, suspended in an "interregnum" between an accomplished past still haunting our memories and an unknown future. What is certain, however, and what marks a substantial difference between past and present, is that fascist movements of the interwar period did not attempt to mainstream, explain or legitimize their activity. Their totalitarianism was ideologically antidemocratic and violent. While nowadays the Right attempts and succeeds in normalizing its discourse

(Berezin, 2011), in the past, despite the fact that fascism got into power through political coalitions, fascists did not feel it was necessary to change their violent totalitarian methods and ideals. As António Costa Pinto (2012, 1) notes, the generic fascism appearing throughout Europe during the first half of the twentieth century was revolutionary, nationalist, anti-Communist and violent.

In that historical context, fascism emerged as a reaction to an unresolved continental conflict, the Great Depression and, most critically, the perceived Communist threat. This dynamic allowed the bourgeoisie to endorse fascist counterrevolutionary violence despite fascism's own anti-bourgeois stance. Today, however, nothing similar occurs. The bourgeoisie largely aligns with the progressive agenda, seeing it as compatible with its own interests, and hardly requires fascism to suppress revolutionary movements that might challenge its position.

So we might conclude that if there is a "fascism of the future," it will not resemble the classical form in outward signs and symbols (Paxton, 2005). Some, such as Jason Stanley (2018), go further in identifying what could be defined as a "fascism of the everyday," present in language and perception and daily normalized. For these latter scholars, then, democracy does not have to break down for it to be subject to a creeping fascistization. The question at hand is whether the notion of "creeping fascistization" or the use of a normalized fascist language serves as a means to evade confronting the reality that a resurgent conservative revolution in contemporary times presents viable and coherent alternatives to the liberal world order. Instead of merely attributing the emergence of a normalized "irrational and violent" language, it is pertinent to consider whether we are witnessing the unfolding of a comprehensive ideological alternative. Other scholars, however, are reluctant to accept the concept of fascism or to define current national populist movements. For Ernst Nolte (1966), Stanley Payne (1996) and James Gregor (2000), fascism is a phenomenon limited to the interwar period. More recent research such as that of Kurt Weyland (2021, 316) even concludes that "if concepts are used with any precision, then observers need not worry about a revival of fascism." As Jeffrey Bale and Tamir Bar-On hint, those using the fascist terminology nowadays are in reality fighting the last war, exploding the threat posed by the domestic radical right in order to censor and cancel disgruntled citizens (Bale and Bar-On, 2022). Moreover, other scholars are reluctant to accept the very idea of a fascist intellectual sphere and, in their view, protofascist intellectuals just created a loose worldview rather than a structured ideology (Mann, 2004, 10, 13). From a methodological perspective, skeptical observers may also cast doubts about the impact of ideas in general. They stress the force of conducive conditions rather than ideas in accounting for institutional reform. However, limiting ourselves to conducive conditions hardly can provide explanations about the substantive content of the revolutionary change (Berman 1998, 16–19; Lieberman, 2002, 697). As Rogers Smith (2001, 73) claims, "the dominant tendency in political science is to minimize the role of such idea-laden narratives." However, if we want to understand, for example, how for more than twenty years, political institutions were open to political correctness, identity politics and post-nationalism, it is worth considering what these ideas are and how they were shaped in different intellectual laboratories before being institutionalized. At this juncture, this Element asserts that a fascist ideological framework in the past preceded the conditions, enabling it to gain political power. Similarly, it contends that a protofascist ideological framework is currently emerging, taking into account the contemporary challenges of modern society. Scholars such as Zeev Sternhell (1995) and James Gregor (2005), among others, have discussed the ideological and cultural roots of fascism. The fascist intellectual sphere, according to Sternhell, goes back to the early twentieth century, before the fascist movements were even created. It could be defined as an intellectual reaction against the scientific and political optimism of the early twentieth century. As Ira Katznelson (2003, 8) correctly described, "Just before the First World War ... the disclosure and invention of knowledge were guided by a profound optimist that reason ... could shine on all aspects of human politics, morality and political economy." In political terms, both liberalism and Marxism, despite their opposition, embodied the two facets of rational optimism toward progress. However, fascism emerged as a force that shattered this utopian optimism. It symbolized a backlash against the ethos of moral and social advancement, and within a shared spirit of resistance to the Enlightenment, we can discern the convergence of seemingly incompatible trajectories. On one side, nationalists like Maurice Barrès and Charles Maurras rejected democratic civic nationalism in favor of anti-bourgeois revolutionary organic nationalism. On the other side were the followers of the Marxist philosopher Georges Sorel, who challenged the foundational tenets of Marxism by rejecting the traditional conflict between the proletariat and bourgeoisie. Instead, Sorel redefined class struggle as a battle between the productive elements of the proletariat nation – such as workers and investors – and nonproductive entities like financial capital and the idle bourgeoisie. The synthesis between left and right was specially reflected in Georges Sorel's *Reflexions sur la violence* (1908), which promoted the idea that revolutionary syndicalism should endorse the myth of the nation. According to Sternhell, during the early years of the twentieth century, that synthesis forged at the Cercle Prouhdon developed a "third way" of political modernization rooted in a Sorelian and Nietzschean vitality (Sternhell, Sznajder and Asherri, 1994). The model was copied in Italy, where nationalists such as Gabriele d'Annunzio and Enrico Corradini and socialists like Benito Mussolini understood that nationalism and socialism should unite. As defined by the Italian socialist Arturo Labriola already in 1910, there were two types of nationalism: the nationalism of the workers – popular and equalitarian – and the nationalism of the elites – dishonest and imperialist (Sternhell, Sznajder and Asherri, 1994, 250). The nationalism of the workers represented a voluntarist view of politics interpreted as a voice of liberation (Beiner, 2018, 16). Interestingly, the emerging voice of liberation did not align with the Bolshevik Communist movement but opposed it. This new figure – the nationalist worker – rejected the universal and moral principles of both Marxism and liberalism, instead adopting a national-racist stance against what was seen as the moral and cultural decadence in both ideologies.

This leads to an inquiry into the enduring core goals of fascism, which persist despite its defeat in the world war (Freeden, 1996). Is that left–right synthesis relevant in current times? In what way? According to Roger Griffin and several other scholars, there is indeed a continuation of the main fascist synthesis whose main goal is to elevate the community out of the ashes of a decadent society. This is a configuration that Griffin (2000, 165) defines as a "palingenetic ultra-nationalism." Roger Eatwell (1996, 303) argues that "generic fascism, transcending place and time, is ... an ideology that strives to forge social rebirth based on a holistic-national radical Third Way." We argue that precisely this "third way" is repeated with full strength in current times, characterized by its rejection of the spirit of triumphalist liberalism. As Sternhell (2008, 280) noted, "thinking about fascism is not a reflection on a regime or a movement but a reflection on the risks that might be involved for a whole civilization when it rejects the notion of universal values, when it substitutes historical relativism for universalism, and substitutes various communitarian values for the autonomy of the individual."

Many critics would likely challenge Sternhell's position. Indeed, a radical critique of the Enlightenment's political ideals is embraced by a diverse range of liberal, conservative and left-wing theorists and scholars who have no connection to fascism. Yet, historically, fascism did represent an extreme form of anti-Enlightenment sentiment. Today, so-called post-fascism – which we describe as a "new fascism of resistance" – embodies a renewed defiance against Enlightenment values. This resistance is also directed at what post-fascist thinkers frame as a colonialist agenda embedded in the doctrine of universal human rights, which they perceive as a tool of cultural and political imposition.

The ideological elaboration of this new fascism of resistance has been underway for more than three decades at intellectual laboratories in Europe and America. This was a metapolitical strategy that was largely at the fringes of the theoretical debate for most of that time. Nowadays, however, it comes to the surface, bringing precise content to the new "politics of rage" against liberal elites and their globalizing project.

2.1 The Ideological Construction of a Fascism of Resistance: Conservative Revolution, Traditionalism and Right-Wing Postcolonialism

To comprehend the emergence of what we term as a fascism of resistance, it is imperative to analyze the convergence between the principles of the new conservative revolution and the neo-Traditionalist current. The Weimar conservative revolution of the interwar period has been of special attraction for the members of the New Right. Gathered around universities, political clubs and journals such as *Die Tat* (*The Deed*), *Die Standarte* (*The Standard*) and *Das Gewissen* (*Conscience*), a heterogeneous group of nationalist intellectuals such as Arthur Moeller van den Bruck, Hans Freyer, Ernst Junger, Carl Schmitt, Werner Sombart, Martin Heidegger, Ernst Niekisch and Oswald Spengler decided to transform defeated German nationalism into something dynamic and victorious. Despite their differences, these intellectuals promoted this type of modern nationalist mobilization, based on the Schmittian primacy of the political over morality and responsibility. The act of politics itself thus represents the primacy of identity over reason. Echoing Heidegger, they understood that they had to take a risky leap into a new beginning, challenging the familiar understanding of conservatism. A conservative revolution is thus first and foremost a revolution of values. The question, however, is what is conservative about such a conservative revolution? For in principle, nothing seems as far from Edmund Burke's conservatism than a revolutionary mood. Conservatives stick to ancient ways of doing things, combining sentiment and pragmatism. Michael Oakeshott used to remark that conservatives prefer the familiar to the unknown and the tried to the untried, and in general they reject the utopian bliss of liberals (Oakeshott, 1962, 1991, 407–437). However, as Albert Mohler (the Swiss historian of the European new right) explained, we have to consider breakthrough moments in history in order to redefine concepts (Mohler, 1972). Every generation has its own conservatism, which is not readily adaptable by the next one. Even a conservative ideology is therefore dynamic and requires continuous reflection. Germany's defeat in the First World War and the imposition of a liberal democratic system by the winning coalition opened the way to a redefinition of the national question and its relationship with conservative thought. As Jeffrey Herf (1986, 3) has observed, where German conservatives had spoken of technology or culture, the new conservative revolutionaries have conceived of a synthesis between a reactionary tribal identity and an anti-Enlightenment modernism. Indeed, German National Socialism showed the "Janus face" of fascism claims. It is "hostile to western rationalist tradition, deeply nostalgic, and steeped in *volkisch* and agrarian mythology, while also projecting a futuristic utopia" (Gat, 1997, 31). Yet the striking thing, and the reason the post-fascist New Right has reevaluated the role of the Weimar conservative revolution, is that while the latter erected the ideological pillars of National Socialism, several of its members opposed totalitarianism, albeit from a National Socialist perspective. Some of these fascists were persecuted by the Nazis, and others such as Edgar Jung were murdered by them. Ernst Niekisch (1889–1967), a leading proponent of National Bolshevism (a synthesis of planned Soviet socialism and nationalism) and an anti-Semite, rejected Hitler for being insufficiently revolutionary. Heidegger, himself an admirer of National Socialism, still made no compromise with vulgar Nazi populism. Why were these criteria relevant for the precursors of a regenerated fascism? As the neofascist Maurice Bardeche remarked, fascism was "ghettoized" and even imprisoned by a post-Nuremberg liberal political establishment (Bardeche, 1961). That was the time however, when a wide variety of European nationalists understood that the revolutionary ideology of National Socialism was one thing, and its totalitarian conclusions another. For the later fascism was a revolutionary idea that had to be regenerated (Bar-On, 2007; Mammone, 2009). In short, that meant severing fascist revolutionary ideology from totalitarian practices.

The French and European New Right have engaged in this endeavor of revitalizing the revolutionary ideas of the conservative revolution for more than four decades. This intellectual search has served as a crucial pillar in the enhancement of a new revolutionary ethnonational identitarianism. However, the question arises as to whether the ideas originating from the conservative revolution, which laid the groundwork for a third path to modernization, can be reconciled with Traditionalism, an ideological trend that initially appeared to be inherently resistant to revolution and novelty. The first key idea of Traditionalism is that an idealized past that was lost because of moral degeneration and the progressive abandonment of religion should be recovered. Traditionalists thus depict tradition as a concept that indicates the spiritual wisdom that is conceived as having formed the ancient core of all the great religions and spiritual paths: the perennial philosophy (Sedgwick, 2016, 308). This "primordial Tradition" that precedes all local traditions is transmitted from the origin of humanity and then restored (perhaps imperfectly and partially) by authentic founders of new faiths (François, 2014, 97). As such it sets a form of collective consciousness related to the "primordial identity of human communities" (François, 2014, 88). One notable aspect of Traditionalism is its recognition of the interconnectedness of various spiritual paths. By acknowledging the shared wisdom and spiritual heritage across different traditions, Traditionalism promotes a broader perspective that transcends sectarian divides (Faivre, 1996, 68). Leaders within the Traditionalist movement have often explored and appreciated the teachings and insights present in Christianity and Islam, for example.

The French thinker René Guénon ('Abd al-Wahid Yahya, 1886–1951), the Swiss philosopher Frithjof Schuon ('Isa Nur al-Din Ahmad, 1907–1998) and Martin Lings, among others, adopted or converted to Islam. Figures like Schuon even established a Traditionalist *ṭarīqa* (Sufi order), the Maryamiyya. These thinkers generally regarded Islamic traditions, particularly within Sufi orders, as providing more direct access to the spiritual essence that all religions ultimately seek. Although primarily a religious movement, Traditionalism also had significant political and philosophical impact. For instance, Guénon founded the Integralist Traditional school, and Julius Evola (1898–1974) developed what is recognized as the political version of Traditionalism.

Despite their differences, Guénon and Evola both regarded the values arising from the liberal revolutions as responsible for the disintegration of traditional sociopolitical structures, thereby marking the beginning of the end of the West. Both of them believed that it would not be enough to revive forms of societal order from the prerevolutionary past. However, the variances between the two were salient. Julius Evola was initially an admirer of Guénon and shared Guénon's ultratraditionalist and spiritual perspective. However, Evola later radicalized Traditionalism to substantiate his own "super-fascist ideas" (Wolff, 2016, 491). Indeed, through Guénon, Evola alimented his own aspiration to restore a sacred and mythological relation with the national past. He understood that Italy never had a traditionalist government and never defended "foundational principles." Italy, according to Evola, "lacks an authentic 'traditional' past" to restore. Mussolini himself respected Evola and even commissioned him to formulate a "Fascist" spiritual (as opposed to "National Socialist") racial doctrine. Evola himself was an ardent supporter of Mussolini and enjoyed the dubious privilege of having the Duce endorse his book, *Synthesis of the Doctrine of Race* (1941), as the official statement of Fascism's "spiritualist" racism as against Nazism's merely biological racism (Sheehan, 1981, 50). However, Evola's "spiritual racism not only discriminated against the Jews, but all representatives of the modern western world." Up to this juncture, it becomes evident why Evola remained on the periphery of fascist modernism, despite Mussolini's admiration for him. His theories are not aligned with key ideological currents within Fascism such as revolutionary syndicalism, corporatism or national socialism (Wolff, 481). Moreover, as James Gregor (2006, 83–110) remarks, Evola has personally denied he was a fascist, and his elitist theory is deeply aristocratic, nonmodern and un-fascist. Still, despite that, Evola was considered, especially after 1945, the most important Italian theoretician of the so-called conservative revolution.

In this postmodern era, Evola's traditionalism is revered as a fount of inspiration. Against all odds, Evola's concept of spiritual racism or Guénon's integralism and reconciliation with Islam, though unconventional, serve as sources of inspiration for a new theory of right-wing anti-imperialism. This theory could be directed against Islamic imperialism, or conversely, it could use Islam as an example against Western imperialism. Indeed, this perspective challenges conventional assumptions about the New Right as staunch adversaries of Islam. While partially true, as we shall explore, there exist more ambivalences than common assumptions concerning Islam. Guénon himself, although he considered that a full restoration of the Catholic Church was necessary in order to save the West, still believed that if the Catholic Church failed in that mission, a sort of Islamic cultural revolution could be considered as an option. The influential role of Sufi sheiks over Western intellectuality would be essential in that mission.

The West, according to Guénon, has not preserved the mystic esoteric quest as Islam has, especially in its Sufi expression, and has plunged into secularism and barbarism. His paradoxical ensuing conclusion was that Islam could come precisely to save the West from its own destruction. The interesting thing, however, is that he himself did not convert to Islam. For Traditionalists like Guénon, "entering" into Islam was distinct from "conversion," which they viewed as a superficial, exoteric process. Instead, they advocated for learning from the esoteric wisdom of initiated teachings, which allowed individuals to "adopt a traditional form other than that to which they might be linked by their origin" (Guénon, 1975, 104). Indeed what mattered for Guénon was the esoteric part of religion, which is where perennial truth was to be found (Bar-On, 2014, 89). Evola also considered Islam to be connected to the primordialist tradition, and in particular he considered it superior to Christianity and Judaism. For example, he despised the Judaic mercenary character and Christian pietism, which he claimed were the reasons for Western decadence. In his *Revolt against the Modern World* (1995, 245), he theorized Islam's superiority specially in the organizational principle of the social life, regulated by Islamic law. Sharia was revealed directly by God to guide believers in the practical expression of their faith and conduct, whose basis is the Qur'an. In his *The Metaphysics of War* (2007), Evola even portrayed jihad as a "late rebirth of a primordial Aryan heritage" such that the Islamic tradition serves as the transmitter of the Aryo-Iranian tradition (Evola, 2007, 96; Mutti, 2007). Of no doubt Evola was a forerunner in establishing common grounds between fascism and Islamism.

It is of no surprise thus, for example, that fascism and National Socialism displayed an ambivalent approach toward Islam. The question arises as to whether insights gleaned from the particular brand of racist radical nationalism "national socialists" espoused can shed light on why and to what extent they might align themselves with national liberation movements in general and anti-Western religious identities as Islam. This prompts further inquiry into the extent to which they could engage in a shared struggle against liberal colonialism despite being supremacist and imperialist. From an historical perspective, as stressed by David Motadel (2019, 843), "during the Second World War, Berlin became a hub of global anti-imperial revolutionary activism. Between 1941 and 1945, scores of anti-colonial leaders flocked to Germany, among them Indians, most famously Subhas Chandra Bose; prominent Arabs, including the Iraqi nationalist Rashid ʿAli al-Kaylani, the Syrian rebel leader Fawzi al Qawuqji, and Amin al-Husayni, the notorious Mufti of Jerusalem; Irish radicals, such as Seán Russell; and nationalist revolutionaries from Central Asia and the Caucasus – Turkestanis, Azerbaijanis, Chechens, and others." Indeed, many of them saw Germany as an ally in their struggle for a new world order. While it is true that Hitler was hardly interested in the colonies of the countries he conquered (Burbank and Cooper, 2010, 405), he still for pragmatic reasons aided nationalist rebels in their actions against old colonialist states. Furthermore, there was an attempt to organize a radical international against empire, characterized by transnational militancy and anti-colonial solidarity (Motadel, 2019, 844).

From a different perspective, also in Fascist Italy we can see the development of what could be defined as "anti-colonialist imperialism," or what the Italian nationalist Enrico Corradini defined in 1910 as the "imperialism of proletarian nations." According to Corradini (1923, 89), there were proletarian nations just as there are proletarian classes. He claimed that "as Socialism teaches the proletariat the value of class struggle so must we teach Italy the value of international struggle." To be precise, colonial practices during the time of fascism did not differ from the practices of the liberal period. They had never been moved by economical factors but by prestige and state search for power. As the socialist Filipo Turati noted already in 1895, the African enterprise is essentially not a capitalist phenomenon but a militaristic one (Segre, 1979, 175). However, there was more than that, and that was specifically related to the particular status of the Italian state in world competition. During the 1880s and 1890s, the colonialist enterprise had became largely a southern phenomenon because it suggested an obvious solution to the problems of poverty and the massive emigration that had begun around 1885. Indeed, population outlets became the most powerful rationale for overseas expansion. This did not change with fascism, however; ideologically it was presented as a different type of proletarian colonialism.

Furthermore, at the conceptual level of international relations, fascist colonialism in Africa, as well as the Nazi Lebensraum aimed at colonizing Central and Eastern Europe, or, currently, Dugin's theory of Eurasia, all align with the theory of multipolarity expanded by Carl Schmitt. This theory promotes an "anti-imperialist imperialism" or regional zones of influence, and stands in opposition to liberal global colonialism. In Schmitt's telling, the Monroe Doctrine was functionally operating to keep "spatially alien powers" out of the United States' wider sphere of influence in the Americas. This formed the nucleus of Schmitt's thinking about the *Großraum* (great space).

Schmitt's *Großraum* stood in sharp contrast to British imperialism, as the latter rested, at least in theory, on the "universalistic humanitarian concerns" stemming from "individualistic-liberal" premises (von Bogdandy and Hussain, 2021, 152). According to Schmitt, however, it was precisely the might of an Anglo-American commercial and maritime empire that has destroyed the "*jus publicum Europaeum*" that had successfully stabilized relationships between European states for roughly two hundred years. Following this argument, it is easy to understand why post-fascists nowadays portray Russia's Eurasian imperialism and China's expansionism in the South Pacific as legitimate types of imperialism. Indeed, these examples inspired the ideologues of what we define as the postcolonial fascism of resistance, a concept that extends beyond international affairs to influence domestic politics as well. This new concept challenges conventional wisdom, particularly in the context of the typical divide between left-wing and right-wing ideologies, and the associated views on colonialism and imperialism.

2.2 Right-Wing Postcolonialism?

This brings us to a complex and paradoxical intersection: How can right-wing conservative ideologies, which often promote white supremacy, nationalist agendas, and anti-multiculturalism with a disdain for Global South cultures, find any common ground with postcolonialism? One could also ask what potential parallels could be drawn between the fascist concept of "proletarian imperialism," Nazi aspirations to overturn the humiliation of the Treaty of Versailles, and modern revivalist movements such as Islamic resurgence or Iranian Shiite expansionism. In each case, there is a drive to restore perceived lost dignity and counter an imposed sense of weakness or subjugation. Both fascist and postcolonial nationalist ideologies have sought, in different ways, to reclaim pride and sovereignty.

Postcolonial authors, however, would firmly reject any moral or ideological alignment between fascism, Nazism and anti-colonial struggles. Since the 1950s, both Frantz Fanon (1961) and Hannah Arendt (1945) have strongly argued that Western colonialism was a significant, though not exclusive, historical factor in the rise of Hitler's dictatorship in the twentieth century (Bernhard, 2018, 121). They emphasized that fascism was fundamentally entangled with the structures of colonial rule, the racialized organization of dispossession and death, and insatiable imperial ambition. In the aftermath of the Second World War, Aimé Césaire (1950/2000), in *Discourse on Colonialism*, described the "decivilizing" effects of colonialism on the colonizers themselves as a root cause of Nazism and other Euro-American fascisms. Indeed the racial terror and genocide wrought by slavery and colonialism preceded, were constitutive of and continued after Mussolini's Fasci Italiani di Combattimento, the National Socialist German Workers' Party, and Japan's Shōwa nationalism (Goldstein and Trujillo, 2021, 3). Recent scholarship, such as the work of Marianna Griffini, has illuminated the colonialist legacy of fascism within contemporary populist right-wing movements. Griffini contends that the Italian populist radical right-wing anti-immigrant rhetoric, for example, draws from Italy's colonial and fascist past. The lack of a comprehensive postwar reckoning with fascism has, she argues, inhibited the development of critical frameworks for analyzing fascist imperialism and colonialism (Griffini, 2023, 133). The racism evident in parties like La Lega and Fratelli d'Italia can be seen in their discourse on the Mediterranean Sea, which they describe as a zone of "uncontrolled and undesired immigration." This contrasts with the fascist-era term *Mare Nostrum* (Our Sea), which signified ownership and pride in Italy's colonial ambitions. Today, their rhetoric has shifted to a notion of *Mare Vostrum* (Your Sea), embodying an exclusionary mindset that rejects the presence of immigrants in the region (Griffini, 2023).

However, postcolonialist theory not only links fascism to a previous Western colonialism, but also confronts the cultural repercussions of colonialism and imperialism in non-Western societies. According to Gurminder Bhambra, the studies of Edward W. Said (1995), Homi K. Bhabha (1994) and Gayatri Spivak (1988) (projected in the research of the modernity/coloniality school of sociologists such as Anibal Quijano [2007], María Lugones [2007] and the semiotician Walter D. Mignolo [2000]), emphasized the need to consider the emergence of the modern world in the broader histories of colonialism, empire and enslavement promoted by Western societies (Bhambra, 2014, 115).

As scholars like Vivienne Jabri argue, while colonial subjects were once overtly subjected to conquest, in the postcolonial era, power manifests in more covert, regulatory forms. The international arena is reshaped into a cosmopolitan space (Jabri, 2013, 3–4). However, this cosmopolitan ideal often functions as a framework of subjugation for the new postcolonial subjects, the immigrants. As Enzo Traverso (2016) contends, Western democracies' inability to effectively integrate immigrants inevitably fosters exclusion and marginalization (Traverso, 2016, 89). Compounding this issue, Western societies also maintain hierarchical structures that continue to suppress non-Western identities and limit autonomy in non-Western regions, thereby perpetuating a global division that conceals its colonial foundations. At first glance, there thus seems to be little compatibility between what could be defined as the Left's progressive postcolonialism and the post-fascist Right's anti-immigration take on postcolonialism.

Paradoxically, however, the concept of postcolonialism on the Right, as developed by the French New Right, still aligns with certain critiques of Western colonialism typically associated with the Left. Not only does it accept the basic argument that the cosmopolitan break of the international world constitutes the weapon of the resilience of liberal colonialism, but it also adds that in order to resist global liberal values, cultural diversity arguments should be endorsed. The new message is that black people in Africa and white identitarians in Europe are presented as victims of Western universal liberalism and are in need of protection. In this distorted narrative, the "black lives matter" movement in Africa and the "white lives matter" movement in Europe and America are portrayed as brothers in arms. Nobody would express this better than Marcus Garvey, the black neofascist nationalism founder of the Universal Negro Improvement Association, when conducting his propaganda campaigns in the 1920s in the black ghettos with the slogan, "Africa for the Africans, like Asia for the Asians and Palestine for the Jews" (Neuberger, 1996, 20).

In this context, right-wing postcolonialists may even appropriate Jean-Paul Sartre's (2001) argument about black resistance to white racism, which he defined as *"un racisme anti-raciste."* This concept – now being extended to the broader resistance of the Global South to Western modernization and reframed as a form of legitimate defiance against liberal hegemony – has been adopted by the new post-fascists. The post-fascists embracing this interpretation argue that Western colonialism – through the imposition of universal human rights and liberal or socialist models of modernization – has not only colonized the non-European world but also eroded the authentic, rooted identities of European ethnic identities.

Furthermore, by reclaiming the intellectual legacy of various racist anti-colonialists from the past and emphasizing their shared perspectives with

Global South nationalists, the new fascists of resistance seek to redefine postcolonial discourse and identity politics by advocating a shared struggle of the Global South and an ethnic Europe against liberal globalization. This framing casts both economic elites and progressive activists as agents undermining national identities and cultural heritage, with immigration policies seen as a tool to dilute or replace traditional European populations. By framing these groups as allied forces in a perceived cultural and demographic invasion, the populist Right appeals to a defense of national sovereignty and traditional values, painting itself as the last bastion against this so-called colonization of Europe.

This perspective was articulated by Italian prime minister Giorgia Meloni in her response to Emmanuel Macron's strong critique of the Fratelli d' Italia and its anti-immigration stance. Addressing a rally, Meloni said, "What is disgusting is France, which continues to exploit African countries, charging them minting fees, using child labor in the mines, and extracting raw materials, as is happening in Niger. Don't lecture us, Macron. Africans are abandoning their continent because of you." Her conclusion was clear: "The solution is not to bring Africans to Europe, but to liberate Africa from certain Europeans" (Macnulty, 2022).

More importantly from an ideological perspective, an interesting theoretical and political phenomenon emerges here. As George Hull (2022, 131) argues, despite their distinct intellectual lineages, postcolonialists of the Right and the Left converge on their "epistemic ethnonationalism" – a doctrine claiming that the beliefs one should adopt and the concepts one should employ are determined by the *ethnos* or ethnic group to which one belongs. Indeed, the tragedy of left-wing postcolonialism is that it echoes ancestral fantasies of the far Right in which who is allowed to live in which places is a question of the connection of one's blood to a particular patch of soil (Polgreen, 2024). For this reason, it is not surprising that fascists in the past and post-fascists today may adopt anti-colonialist stances from a position of ethnic resistance against global liberalism. As Olivia C. Harrison (2022) explains, "Sixty years after French colonial rule ended in Algeria, the idea of decolonization has also become a buzzword in the arsenal of nativist right-wing groups who have recast it as the right to ethnonational self-determination. In this perverse upending of the very meaning of decolonization, to decolonize France is to rid the nation of the immigrants who are 'colonizing' it." Left-wing postcolonialists fall into this trap. In his "perversity thesis," Albert Hirschman (1991, 7) argues that and radical multiculturalism, which originated as a way to encourage minority communities to resist racism, might lead precisely to their oppression. We could extend this claim also in regards to postcolonialists and their decoloniality theory.

In summary, both right-wing Traditionalists and left-wing postcolonialists reject Western beliefs and the application of Western concepts outside the West.

However, it is Traditionalists, rather than members of the progressive left, who take the conceptual revolution to its extreme consequences. The right proposes a completely new vision for what it argues should be a "free world" emancipated from the Western concept of freedom. Furthermore, as Miri Davidson (2024) suggests, "despite similarities, left-wing decolonialists propose an open pluriverse of entanglement between different social, cultural or ethnic groups or peoples. The New Rightists instead propose a closed pluriverse defined by the separation between such groups."

In short, conservative and right-wing movements often adopt selective, exclusionary forms of anti-globalism and appropriate the language of anti-imperialism, even while it remains somehow incompatible with the ethical foundations of postcolonial and decolonial theory. Yet the New Right has pursued this objective for more than three decades, aiming to apply the narrative of human dignity and emancipation not only to formerly colonized societies, but also to Europe itself, which they portray as needing liberation from what they frame as a liberal, postcolonial hegemony. There is no doubt that the ethical and historical implications of such a claim remain deeply contentious.

3 The French Nouvelle Droite. Between the Conservative Revolution and Traditionalism: Post-fascism and Anti-colonialism

The intellectual origins and evolution of the anti-liberal conservative right in France has a long history. From the days of the Dreyfus Affair, featuring movements such as *L'Action Francaise* (French Action), *Ligue des Patriotes* (League of Patriots), *Les Camelots du Roi* (The King's Camelots) and so on, the French conservative Right has usually been associated with anti-liberalism, anti-Republicanism, anti-Semitism and, later, with collaboration with the Nazis. After the Second World War, the Poujadist movement in the 1950s, or the OAS after Algerian emancipation, and Marine Le Pen's National Front (National Rally) were intimately related to the French far Right. However, the emergence of the Nouvelle Droite (ND) in the 1960s, led by its undisputed figurehead de Benoist, has sparked particular interest. It could be argued that the ND reached its mass-media heyday in France in the late 1970s. Dailies like *Le Figaro* regularly published its articles, and during the ND's "hot summer" of press attention in 1979, "its cultural apogee achieved a tipping point when about 500 articles were written about the ND in the mainstream press alone" (Bar-On, 2001, 34).

The weekly *Le Canard enchaîné* (*The Chained Paper*) was asking as long ago as 1972 whether France was dealing with a neo-Nazi group. The Christian Right, gathered around the Nouvelle Action Royaliste (NAR), defined the ND as a dangerous movement promoting anti-Christian values such as eugenics, paganism and racism (Camus, 2019). However, the most dramatic moment in the saga of the ND came in the early 1990s when a group of forty French intellectuals signed the "Appeal for Vigilance," calling for a boycott of ND-affiliated intellectuals. The question, however, was what was new and frightening about the ND. Indeed, what a wide variety of observers perceived as a threat was the perplexing attempt by the New Right and its intellectual leader de Benoist to modernize, transform and humanize racism. The pressing question thus is how racist exclusionism could be making a comeback, disguised this time as a progressive post-national, anti-colonialist ideology, supposedly supportive of cultural difference. How did it happen? This is what the ideological evolution of the ND helps us to understand.

Already in the 1960s, young right-wing activists, members of groups such as Europe-Action, the Federation of Nationalist Students (FEN) and the Rassemblement Européen pour la liberté (REL), understood that their old ultra-nationalist and anticommunist beliefs, centered on scientific racism and eugenics, had became outdated and needed to be adjusted to new realities and to new intellectual and ideological debates. Similar to the New Left that in the 1960s had criticized Soviet Marxism in the name of a humanist Marxism, the New Right appeared to be criticizing old-style racial Nazism in the name of a libertarian "national-socialism" and a pluralist "differentialism" (Taguieff, 1994; Spektorowski, 2012). Simultaneously, they were critical of current conservatism and of economic neoliberalism. By the end of the 1960s, people such as de Benoist, together with a number of followers such as Jacques Bruyas, Guillaume Faye, Jean Jacques Mourreau and Dominique Venner, founded the *Groupement de Recherche et d'Etude pour la Civilization Européenne* (Research and Study Group for European Civilization [GRECE]), a new laboratory of ideas a place where a "revolution of the Right" was to take place and then expand across Europe. Self-defined as "Gramscians of the Right," de Benoist and friends had in mind a metapolitical strategy rather than direct political action (Venner, 1993). Indeed, like Gramsci, they held that revolutionary change occurs not through traditional parliamentary or extraparliamentary confrontation (a "war of movement"), but rather through "a war of position" – a more protracted, deeper process of constructing a new ideology that resonates with and yet modifies "common sense," forming the basis for a counterhegemonic project (Abrahamsen et al., 2020, 95).

As de Benoist (1979b, 19) noted, "without a precise theory, there is no effective action ... The right in France hasn't realized yet the importance of Gramsci. It hasn't seen that cultural power threatens the apparatus of the state." The project was copied in Germany by the Thule Seminar (whose name recalls the Thule Society with its strong links to the early Nazi Party) led by Pierre Krebs and Armin Mohler. In Italy, the New Right was associated with Pino Rauti, one of the ideological leaders of the Movimento Sociale Italiano/ Alleanza Nazionale, and with publications such as *La Destra*, *La Voce della Fogna*, *Diorama Letterario*, *Trasgression* and *Elementi* edited by one of the main ideologues of the Lega Nord, Marco Tarchi. Furthermore, publications such as *The Scorpion*, edited by Michael Walker in England; *Orientation* and *Vouloir*, edited by Robert Steuckers in Belgium, and the magazines *Tekos-Tekste* and *Kommentaren*, edited by Luc Pauwels in the Flanders region, are proof of the scope of the intellectual spirit of the ND, whose first goal was to disassociate itself from the liberal Right. During the 1970s, de Benoist determined that his mission was to penetrate mainstream political and cultural journals in an attempt to refashion center-Right parties and ideologies. The reason was that the liberal Right, the neo-Gaullist Rassemblement pour la République, (Rally for the Republic) and the moderate, right-of-center Union pour la Démocratie française limited themselves to being anticommunists while defending promarket values and the expansion of liberal democracy.

At that critical juncture, de Benoist advocated for these forums to relinquish their dedication to fundamental values like liberty, democracy and Judeo-Christian principles, and to prioritize national identity. His proposal at the beginning garnered partial acceptance from the conservative Right. Indeed, the latter also believed in the possibility of aligning identitarian concerns with economic liberalism, proposing a nativist promarket identitarian agenda. Some members of Giscard's center-Right party, for example, assumed that de Benoist and GRECE would align with the agenda of the ultraliberal think tank Club de l'Horloge, founded in 1974 by senior civil servants associated with GRECE such as Yvan Blot, Henry de Lesquen and Jean-Yves Le Gallou.

However, de Benoist (1990, 15–16; 1991, 3) later on rejected this option, asserting that neoliberal economics and communitarian solidarity are hardly compatible. After distancing themselves from neoconservative ideology, the next step was to develop a new theory of emancipation for the white man and white culture from multiethnic society without succumbing to racism. The initial theoretical move was to challenge the notion of cultural homogenization, which de Benoist argued was the inevitable consequence of homogenizing egalitarianism and human rights ideology, which are the basis of liberal cultural colonialism. "The gradual homogenization of the world [is] advocated and realized by the 2,000-year-old discourse of egalitarian ideology," writes de Benoist (1979b, 19). Moreover, the idea of natural human rights independent of a community is a weapon used by powerful nations to dominate weaker states (de Benoist, 2011a). "The West's conversion to universalism has been the main cause of its subsequent attempt to convert the rest of the world: in the past, to its religion [the Crusades] ... today to its moral principles [human rights]" (de Benoist and Champetier, [1999] 2012).

These principles are propounded by monotheistic religions, which are the basis of modernism. In contrast to monotheistic religion, the New Right defends Traditionalism, which is holistic and antimodern. Nostalgia for "primordial tradition" is projected onto Indo-European paganism, Europe's medieval traditions and Hindu and even Muslim societies (Bar-On, 2014, 87). "Tradition" thus connotes the ongoing transmission of cultural content in a historical processes linked to a founding event or to an immemorial past and folklore inherited from the national past. The impact of Traditionalism for the New Right came precisely from the writings and the political activism of Guénon and especially from Evola, who, according to de Benoist (and contrary to the other theoreticians of Tradition from Guénon to Schuon), constantly took positions on political problems.

> Evola strove to always remain at the level of what for him is essential. . . . It is known that for Evola all of human history, for the last two and a half millennia, can be read as a process of involution. The decadence of the western world is characterized by the progressive loss of the spiritual, virile, and heroic element, which is proper to the "Light of the North," and by the correlative rise of the dissolving values of the "gynecocratic" cultures of the South. (de Benoist, 2003, 6)

It is clear that de Benoist belongs with those New Right members who were seduced by Nordic Traditionalism. Indeed, members of the New Right in general, especially of its *völkisch* wing, were differentialist racists who believed that Nordicism implies a return to the supposed origins of Nordic Indo-Europeans, the "Indigenous people" of Europe. Nordicism expressed through Germanic, Scandinavian and Celtic gods is a vital component of de Benoist's paganism and traditionalism. De Benoist argues that the image of the pagan (*païen*) embodies a contrasting spirit to that of a managerial society and of cosmopolitanism (Benoist, 1981). Furthermore, he constructs his racist differentialist ideology around the image of the Nordic pagan while simultaneously extolling the South as partners in the same struggle for identity. As Taguieff argues, the category of communitarian or differentialist racism, as expounded by de Benoist, differs from universal racism because it does not promote a universal scale of values against which the aptitudes of races can be determined. But the differentialist imperative does divide the human race into cultural totalities (Taguieff 1988).

Each culture should find in its difference the source of new norms and should keep to its own traditional environment, where its full potential can be developed. Unlike French Republican secular assimilationists, de Benoist respects cultural differences. Against all odds for a right-wing exclusionist, de Benoist advocated the right of Muslim schoolgirls to wear a *foulard* (headscarf) during the second *foulard* affair in 2004, a seeming incongruity for a racist. What de Benoist had in mind, however, was not the defense of Muslim girls but a demand that authentic European identitarians wake up and celebrate their own traditions and their own differentialism.

At the theoretical level, de Benoist implies that he is not against Islam or against colored people, but in favor of white people. We "have the right to [be in favor] of black power, but on the condition of simultaneously being in favor of white power, yellow power and red power" (de Benoist, 1979a, 156). Unlike other prominent figures of the New Right, such as Guillaume Faye, who was a leading member of GRECE from 1970 to 1986 and who advocated for the expulsion of Muslims from France, and differing from Renaud Camus's theory of "the great replacement" (Camus, 2011; Faye, 2016), de Benoist disapproves of expulsion. Instead, he advocates for mutual segregation. It is clear to all, however, that mutual segregation would finally lead to the expulsion of the non-Europeans. In other words, despite the widely known mutual abhorrence between de Benoist and Faye, both lead to the same direction. What Faye fails to understand is that his exclusionary strategy and de Benoist inclusion/exclusion strategy are complementary. It could be said that the latter strategy, rather than leading to a multicultural society, encourages the establishment of a multicultural world. In that multicultural world, Muslims should develop their own possibilities and morality in *Dar al Islam* (the lands of Islam), and authentic Europeans should master and connect to their own regional environment and their constitutional myth, deeply rooted in its historical narrative. Similar to Evola, he was critical of non-European peoples renouncing "their traditions, which date back for ages," and have "Westernized, adopting the culture, ideologies, political forms and lifestyles of White peoples" (Evola, 2013, 27, 98).

De Benoist thus posits that "authentic" Europeans stand on equal footing with non-Europeans. However, the perverse conclusion of this mutual recognition and possible cooperation in a common struggle against world liberalism is that Europe and the Global South should have the freedom to safeguard their respective cultures and exercise the liberty to segregate those they deem as inauthentic. Both groups, however, each in its own environment, should collaborate in a struggle against a common foe: the colonialism of the global regime of human rights. These conclusions stem from de Benoist's prompt realization that the progressive Left, having veered decisively away from color-blind egalitarianism, secularism and assimilation and toward cultural diversity, communitarianism and federalism, not only undermines the egalitarian ideology of human rights, but it indirectly contributes to the exclusionary ideology of the right (Camus and Labourg, 2017, 123–124).

In other words, rather than rejecting Will Kymlicka's (1995) liberal multiculturalism or Iris Young's (1990) differential citizenship, he radicalizes their ideas to their bitter end, transforming them from inclusionary to exclusionary. In his *Manifesto for a European Renaissance* ([1999b] 2012), he presents himself as an advocate of cultural diversity in a manner that would resonate with any Anglo-Saxon supporter of multiculturalism: "The true wealth of the world is first and foremost the diversity of its cultures and peoples" (De Benoist and Champetier, [1999b] 2012). Moreover, he attacks the antiracism of egalitarian republicans. The "more the anti-racism is believed in, the more it appears like a racism classically defined as the negation or radical devaluation of group identity" (de Benoist, 2014, 13).

De Benoist's vision, however, is that real cultural diversity requires European culture to assert itself. A world of diversity can thus be propounded by reshaping a National Socialist tradition as pan-European resistance to neoliberal globalization, a European equivalent to the Global South's own struggle against Western colonialism. European emancipation from colonialism implies a rejection of immigration, which de Benoist analyzes through a Marxist lens. In the ND manifesto, *The French New Right for the Year 2000*, de Benoist and Charles Champetier write: "By reason of its rapid growth and its massive proportions, immigration such as one sees today in Europe constitutes an undeniably negative phenomenon ... Immigration is not desirable for the immigrants, who are forced to abandon their native country ... nor is immigration beneficial for the host population receiving the immigrants" (de Benoist and Champetier, [1999a] 2012).

Adopting a left-wing anticapitalist position, de Benoist (2011b) adds that "whoever criticizes capitalism while approving immigration whose working class is its first victim, had better shut up. Whoever criticizes immigration while remaining silent about capitalism should do the same." The solution however, is not universal liberalism or socialism, but nationalism. How, though, can nationalism fit into a postnational world? While the first Weimar conservative revolution prepared the ground for a total deconstruction of democracy and the imperialist world dominance of Western Aryans, the current conservative revolution seems to be aiming at reestablishing the ethnonationalist basis of democracy. At the global level, it fosters a transformation of a liberal world governance into an anti-imperialist region-based distribution of power. Unlike right-wing Euroskeptic nationalists, de Benoist advocates for a new form of Europeanism, pushing an identitarian agenda that transcends traditional nationalism. In a double move, it propounds the end of Western colonialism, together with a resolute avoidance of postcolonial guilt.

The question is who should be considered as "authentic Europeans" who had been colonized, and how do they relate to current existing national identities in a postnationalist Europe? His position indeed could be considered neither left-wing nor right-wing.

In reality, in a very sophisticated way, de Benoist blurs the differences between the progressive Left and the exclusionist Right. In his 1978 prize-winning book *Vu du Droite* (*View from the Right*), he writes that "for the time being, the ideas supported in this work are to the right; they are not necessarily of the right. I can still quite easily imagine some situation where they could be to the left" (de Benoist, 1979b, 2). In general terms, he defines himself as a communitarian like Charles Taylor or Michael Sandel (de Benoist, 1994c, 195). Yet this oscillation between the ideological positions of the left and the right in de Benoist's work might be reminiscent of Sternhell's characterization of a pre-fascist ideological development. De Benoist however, explicitly challenges Sternhell's definition of a pre-fascist ideological development. "In itself, this is a debatable thesis. The expression 'pre-fascism' is ... totally arbitrary, ... a 'theological anachronism'" (de Benoist, 2007, 81). Despite de Benoist's assertions, however, he arguably stands as one of the foremost and most brilliant proponents of the resurrection of the pre-fascist Left–Right synthesis. He is indeed a forerunner of a postcolonialism of the Right, which, in his perspective, evolves from a reinvigorated ethno-European identity.

3.1 Rebuking Liberal Colonialism: The Rise of "Indigenous" European Identities

Most liberals observing the current uprising of populist movements in Europe tend to understand the phenomenon as a nationalist attack on the European Union. As we shall try to demonstrate, however, the ideas advanced against the liberal cosmopolitan union are based on a nationalism that is Europe-centered. More specifically, the New Right strives to synthesize ethnodemocratic entities at the regional level with the idea of a strong European empire, namely a confederation of ethnic regions able to compete on the global level.

First and foremost, it must be stressed that de Benoist considers ethnoregional nations, defined primarily in cultural, social and anthropological terms, as the basis for real democracy. De Benoist is clear that without cohesion at the local level there is no democracy. "The proper functioning of both Greek and Icelandic democracy was the result of cultural cohesion and a sense of shared heritage" (de Benoist, 1995, 75). According to de Benoist, in Europe, the original peoples are Basques, Catalans, Flemings and Scots, and they constitute the basis for the emergence of an authentic nativist ideology combining homogeneous ethnic communities (*ethnos*) and rule by the people (*demos*) (de

Benoist 1991, 95; Bar-On, 2008, 340). Indeed de Benoist as well as a wide variety of right-wing intellectuals such as Gianfranco Miglio, one of the ideological mentors of the Lega Nord, consider the ethnoregional nations harbingers of a whole European cultural renaissance in the face of the ruined modern world (Mammone, 2009, 230).

This particular form of the imagined community, however, cannot be reduced to current understandings of the nation. It strongly rejects the French republican type of assimilationist nationalism, which turns "others" into citizens. Nationality thus cannot be defined by modern statecraft but by nativism. As Guillaume Faye (2010, 12), one of the most radical members of the ND, interpreted it, the basic idea of all rightists old or new is the fact that European nationalism must defend "the native members of a people."

Yet, how those natives should be politically organized is a matter of debate. It is clear that in current world politics, the very idea of narrow sovereignty does not make sense. However, is the European Union the solution? For de Benoist, "the new European political unity cannot be built on the national Jacobin model ... and it cannot ... result from the economic supra-nationality dreamt of by Brussels technocrats" (de Benoist 1994b). The only way Europe can survive politically is to shift down from the obsolete nation-state to ethnoregional identities at the local level, and to shift up to an antiliberal confederation of ethnic regions at the higher level. That means that from a geopolitical and ideological perspective, de Benoist considers pan-European unity "an absolute necessity."

This trend was conceptually elaborated by Armin Mohler, whose main thesis was that the German tradition of the *Reich* (realm) in Central Europe (*Mitteleuropa*) includes two contradictory streams, which at the end of the day complement each other. The first is the idea that the *Reich* symbolizes diversity and decentralization of power with open or at least vaguely defined borders, and the second is an almost mythical view affirming the organic spiritual unity of the *Reich* and *Mitteleuropa* (Mohler, 1972, 139). This *völkisch* (folk or nationalist) pluralism, stressing the unique origins and yet common roots of a putative European culture, was promoted in the 1920s by the Thule Society and partially adopted by the Nazis. In different ways, intellectuals such as Heidegger, Evola and Jean Thiriart have endorsed this view that cannot be identified to narrow nationalism. According to Ronald Beiner, Heidegger's *Dasein*, namely the metaphysical destiny of the German people, for example cannot be reduced just to the predilection for one's own nation (Beiner, 2018, 69).

What worried Heidegger was that liberal society lacked rootedness in an *ethnos*. The question for him was: How could that *ethnos* be represented by current states or by the vulgar homogenizing republican nation? Heidegger was precise in this point. There cannot be a society emerging out of a rational association of individuals but only a community of a *Volk* based on a historically handed-down determination (Heidegger, 2009, 139). That interpretation was shared by Evola, who would reject republican homogenizing nationalism, advocating instead the idea of an organic pagan and hierarchical *imperium*, which could take various forms according to local condition. Indeed, according to Evola (1986, 18, 20), the "European nations have been the very ones that have maintained European disunity from the Hundred Years War to the present day." Evola thus became a supporter of a Europe in which a new version of state and empire could result from the symbiosis of the Roman and Germanic heritage (Griffin, 1995, 343).

Following this line, the New Right historian Pierre Vial wrote in a 1970 article in *Le Monde* that "Fighting for a cultural renaissance, GRECE intended to help establish a founding myth: that of a sovereign, liberated Europe, facing an imperial destiny" (Duranton Crabol, 1988, 99). These ideas were adopted and re-elaborated by a wide variety of right-wing exclusionists related to the New Right.

Jean Thirirat, an ex-Nazi collaborator who after the war founded the group Jeune Nation, wrote a leading document for the New Right, *Un empire de 400 millions d'hommes: L'Europe*, fostering the idea of a new Europe led by an elitist and de-bureaucratized socialism. This would be a hyper nation-state able to compete with the new American Carthage and the billion-strong population of China, and make common cause with the Global South. Even nationalists like Carl Schmitt had, before the end of the war, already devised the idea of the *Großraum*, through which he attempted to reconcile universe and "pluriverse" by suggesting that the state form should be overcome by grand territorial units. In short, argues de Benoist (1994d, 14), a federalism from below, built on the principle of subsidiarity in Europe, is the counterforce to "universalism and national homogenization." This federalism should also contrast with the European Union rooted in the Maastricht Treaty.

According to de Benoist's critique of the Maastricht Treaty framework, the market is viewed as the principal architect of economic identity. Conversely, he advocates for an ethnic federation of peoples, a concept that prioritizes ethnocultural values over economic considerations (de Benoist, 1996, 135). Furthermore, he argues that such an ethnic federation fosters a new form of internationalism, one that stands in stark contrast to liberal internationalism.

Pablo de Orellana and Nicholas Michelsen (2019, 749) claim that the New Right is "defined by an internationalism of its own, which advocates linking nationalist movements to restructure international relations norms." That is indeed true; however, we stress that the New Right's internationalism is built upon a postnational European ethnoregionalism rather than upon an old conservative nationalism.

This move attracted the interest of Paul Piccone, a former editor of the American left-wing journal *Telos*, who perceived the power of ethnoregional populism as presented by de Benoist and the New Right as the only alternative to the technocratic new class leading the liberal world. Indeed, Piccone stresses that a distinction must be made between a liberal Europe embodied in the Maastricht federalism, and right-wing federalism defined as integral federalism (Piccone, 1991). Different from Hamiltonian federalism, which emphasized institutional and constitutional integration, right-wing federalism relies upon a loose confederation of ethnic peoples. By this criterion, while liberal Europe could develop from a Europe of nation-states into a political and economic union resting on the same philosophical basis that is theoretically posited on the primacy of the individual, the integral version of federalism remains a Schmittean version of *Großraum* or an Evolan concept of integral empire, a confederation of ethnic peoples and regions within which aliens and minorities would not have the right to be democratic agents.

Already in the winter of 1991–1992, *Telos* published several articles on regional populism written by the intellectual leader of the Lega Nord, Gianfranco Miglio (1991–1992), as well as by Bernard Poche and Roberto Borcio. It is evident to all that these views do not align with those of the former French National Front. Marine Le Pen and her father both advocate for a sovereign France, a position that differs from de Benoist's perspective. In a similar vein, de Benoist (2021) rejects Eric Zemmour's Jacobinism, particularly his advocacy for assimilation, which is perceived as hostile to regional identities.

The question arises as to why de Benoist contends that ethnoregional identities are antiliberal. It should be apparent that not all groups with strong ethnoregional identities, such as Catalans, Basques and Scots, are antiliberal. However, in de Benoist's view, any synthesis between liberal and organic nationalism is destined to result in the predominance of nationalism over liberalism. This perspective suggests that de Benoist believes the core values and priorities of ethnoregional identities will ultimately conflict with and override liberal principles.

As noted, for both American leftists such as Paul Piccone and rightists such as de Benoist, the exclusionist organic ethnic regions represent a response to liberal globalization and homogenization. Moreover, the struggle of ethnic identities such as Catalans or Flemish against the assimilationist democratic state should be presented on the same footing as any Global South colonized people fighting against imperialism.

Finally, we should be concerned about the feasibility of conflating racist differentialism, ethnoregionalism and anti-colonialism into a singular framework.

Indeed, it seems counterintuitive that peoples from colonized Global South nations would draw inspiration from the organic racist nationalists of the colonial powers. However, historical precedents provide glimpses into some unexpected methods of addressing the issues of colonialism and anti-colonialism, suggesting that the interaction between these ideologies can produce complex and sometimes surprising alignments and narratives (Taguieff, 1988).

And yet some examples from the past allow us to catch a glance of some unexpected ways to deal with the question of colonialism and anti-colonialism. It is clear to all that despite the Third Republic's colonialist zeal, advocated by Alexis de Tocqueville himself, among others, France's democratic republicans such as Georges Clemenceau and Jean Jaurès leaned on their democratic commitments to reject colonialism.

In general terms, left-wing theories opposing colonialism and advocating for respect for minorities are well established. The question, however, is why racist and exclusionist ideologues of the past also expressed anti-colonialist critiques, and what motivated their opposition. It is an apparent anomaly and mostly ignored. But national exclusionists such as Maurice Barrés, while not being anti-colonialist, still rejected the mercantilist colonialism of the Third Republic. He was skeptical of "enlightened" domination of other countries.

De Benoist (1999, 17) expands on this point and claims that while racism has often accompanied and encouraged colonialism, racist beliefs have sometimes also played the opposite role: "Gobineau vigorously denounced all forms of colonialism. . . . Le Bon, who believed in racial inequality, was one of the staunchest opponents of colonial expansion." Furthermore, de Benoist also understood that Gustave Le Bon was an Arabophile. He defended the identity and independence of the Arabs and even considered an alliance between Europe and the Arabs in order to fight Judaism, which at that time was perceived as a harbinger of universal values and the Enlightenment (Spektorowski, 2023, 110–111).

What, then, of the colonized? Madagascar's Jean-Joseph Rabearivelo, thought of as Africa's first modern poet, not only resisted French colonial rule with ferocity, but paradoxically also found political affinities with organic nationalists such as Charles Maurras. Similarly, Leopold Senghor, the outstanding African apostle of Negritude, was deeply influenced by the philosophy of Barrés. The glorification of ethnic customs and rural life by contrast with the impersonality of urban life was central to Barrés and Senghor. Senghor can be portrayed as a Global South nationalist of the capitalist periphery, and Barrés is considered a French racist organic nationalist. The innovation advanced by the New Right, however, is that both are presented on the same footing as cultural emancipators (Spektorowski, 2023). For de Benoist and the New Right, "Europe of its peoples," which embodies an exclusionary ethnonationalist spirit, thus shares common ground with the aspirations of the old Global South in their joint struggle against liberal globalization. The next question is whether and how the New Right's idea of a regional confederation fits Russian imperial interests, and why this is important.

3.2 From Europe des Peoples to the Euro-Asian Empire: From de Benoist to Aleksander Dugin

The links between de Benoist, Faye and other members of the New Right and the Russian Aleksander Dugin are part of a long-standing pattern in which French right-wing nationalists find inspiration in Russia. French antiliberal nationalists used to portray Russia as the last beacon and stronghold of traditional values. For French nationalists, Russia has a mission – to oppose the decaying religions and societies of the West and regenerate Europe through its influence and example (Camus, 2015, 80–81). From here, the French interest in Dugin is not strange. Dugin, a former member of the National Patriotic Front (Pamyat), the anti-Semitic organization of the Perestroika era, has dedicated his intellectual career precisely to stress nationalist cultural regeneration. The question, however, is how important his political role was and what the meaning of nationalist regeneration was.

Scholars such as Timothy Snyder are reluctant to emphasize Dugin's influence in Russian nationalism. Vladislav Surkov, a follower of Ivan Iylin (1882–1954), the prophet of Russian fascism, is probably more influential than Dugin. He was one of the most famous figures helping to shape Russia's master narrative as a sovereign, illiberal democracy (Snyder, 2018, 46–47). However, Dugin still could be considered an enclave character, a puzzling bridge between the European conservative revolution's ideas on empire and Russian's narrow nationalism. In more sense than one, at their core, many of Dugin's works are an amalgamation of Traditionalist concepts, Evola's theories, geopolitical ideas and the ideology of the German interwar "Conservative Revolution" (Shekhovtsov and Umland, 2009, 665).

Dugin's intellectual career started when he joined the underground Yuzhinsky literary circle led by the mystical writer, poet and translator Evgenii Golovin. At the Yuzhinsky circle he encountered Western antiliberal thought, as well as a wide variety of trends in Russian society such as esotericism, integral traditionalism and fascist mysticism (Shekhovtsov, 2015, 35). As early as 1993, he founded, with Eduard Limonov, the National Bolshevik Party (NBP), in line with the ideas of the conservative revolution, especially of Ernst Niekisch who was one of its prominent members. As Andrei Rogatchevski (2007, 90) aptly notes, the NBP can be described as "the most left-wing among the right-wing parties and the most right-wing among the left-wing parties." Dugin aligns closely with this perspective, which he further develops in his *The Fourth Political Theory*. In this work, Dugin argues that the revival of values from the old conservative revolution is a reaction to the total or partial failures of the three dominant political ideologies of recent history – liberal capitalism, communism and fascism. Dugin (2009, 19) stresses that "the form which all three political theories took in the twentieth century is no longer useful, effective, or relevant. They lack the ability to explain contemporary reality or to help us understand current events, and are incapable of responding to the new global challenges."

While it is true that Dugin seeks to transcend all dominant ideologies, he aligns more closely with fascism than with communism or capitalism (Beiner, 2015, 1). However, being aligned with fascism does not equate to fully endorsing fascist ideology. One could argue that, like de Benoist, Dugin espouses a critical theory of fascism. Andrea Umland, for instance, notes that Dugin draws upon the ideas of Evola, who criticized interwar fascism – especially Italian Fascism – for being too moderate and for compromising with traditional elites. Reflecting this critique, Dugin has expressed the most admiration for the Nazi-supported North Italian Social Republic of Salò (1943–1945), which he viewed as fulfilling all the criteria of a true "Third Way" (Umland, 2007, 155; Shekhovtsov and Umland, 2009, 665)

According to Dugin, a revolutionary new way is becoming viable because, despite liberalism's victories over fascism in 1945 and communism in 1991, it has now reached a dead end, mired in what he terms a "nihilistic postmodern stage." He proposes an alternative model that seeks to redefine progress, moving away from both liberal and socialist interpretations. Dugin's vision centers on a return to deeper existential and cultural roots, advocating a new form of geopolitical and civilizational alignment that breaks with the Western tradition of individualistic, materialist progress.

Dugin positions his philosophy as transcending the confines of liberal individualism, racism and nationalism by promoting a return to the essential nature of human self-awareness, drawing on Heidegger's concept of *Dasein*. He argues that this existential reawakening offers a way out of the nihilism and materialism that he associates with modern liberalism. Through this reorientation, Dugin envisions a foundation for future political orders grounded in a profound spiritual and existential framework, one that rejects Western liberalism's prioritization of the individual in favor of a more collective, rooted sense of being.

Dugin might initially appear as a postmodern critic of liberalism, but in *The Fourth Political Theory*, he argues that it is, in fact, Western liberalism that has become postmodern. His critique targets postmodern liberalism, with a particular emphasis on its alignment with globalism and the technological revolution that supports it (Dugin, 2009, 18). It is easy to track that Dugin echoes Heidegger, who "bitterly hated liberalism, viewing it as an expression of 'calculative thinking,' which underlies 'Western nihilism'" (29).

For both Dugin and Heidegger, liberalism represents a mechanistic, rootless ethos that undermines authentic cultural identities and traditional values. In Dugin's view, this "rootless" liberalism epitomizes the postmodern condition, manifesting in globalization, which he links to social and technological phenomena such as "transgender operations, unisexual marriage, and clone production." He sees these developments as part of a distorted reality shaped by mass media and financial speculation, which he argues lack solid economic foundations (Dugin, 2015).

Dugin dismisses the centrality of the individual and embraces Friedrich Nietzsche's critique of progress, yet diverges from Nietzsche by affirming that God remains an active force in guiding Creation. Drawing on Nietzsche's *Thus Spoke Zarathustra*, Dugin argues that man should be overcome, and, inspired by Heidegger, he centers his philosophy on the concept of the "other beginning" – a focal point he considers the most significant aspect of Heidegger's intellectual legacy. As Jeff Love and Michael Meng note, through his voluminous writings on Heidegger, *The Last God*, Dugin attempts to turn Heidegger's "dismantling of the Western metaphysical tradition" into a call for renewal (Dugin 2014a). Indeed Dugin seeks to lead this fight just as Heidegger sought to lead it in the 1930s (Love and Meng, 2017, 307). The "other beginning," as Dugin envisions it, entails breaking free from the dominance of Western thought, which he regards as depleted – especially in its manifestations as liberal democracy and the purported neoliberal technocratic consensus.

Central to Dugin's critique of liberal materialism is Heidegger's notion of *Machenschaft* – a "regime of forgetfulness" characterized by unreflective, materialist, technocratic production. Dugin repurposes this idea to underscore his view of the West as trapped in a cycle of relentless technological advance, which he believes lacks philosophical depth or spiritual grounding. For Dugin, this mechanistic process reflects the Western world's profound detachment from existential meaning.

America stands at the epicenter of this process, though, according to Heidegger, Soviet Russia embodied similar characteristics. In *Introduction to Metaphysics*, Heidegger infamously names two nihilistic epicenters of technocratic modernity: "Russia and America, seen metaphysically, are both the same: the same hopeless frenzy of unchained technology and of the rootless organization of the average man" (Heidegger, 2014, 41). However, while Russia is culturally profound and rooted to the soil (*bodenstiindig*), America is soulless. It is the managerial country by definition and as such it leads the world to its destruction.

Dugin fully embraces these concepts, emphasizing that the Americanization of the world reveals the West as both supremely powerful and on the verge of collapse (Dugin 2014b). From this, Dugin concludes that America and the West are driven solely by blind power, possessing no enduring authority beyond sheer force. However the triumph of force, and of technology as the handmaiden of force, are signs of ultimate decadence and aridity (Love and Meng, 2017). According to Dugin, Russian civilization today represents a form of salvation.

In *The Fourth Political Theory*, Dugin redefines freedom, contrasting it with the liberal conception rooted in individual rights and the protection of "the small man." Instead, he champions the rights of the "great man" – a figure grounded in Heideggerian notions of Being and Time. This "great man" is envisioned as one who asserts authority and imposes order by fulfilling meaningful tasks as well as the taming of the restless and exciting horizons of the will (Dugin, 2012, 51–52).

Thomas Main (2018, 222) insightfully argues that Dugin's political vision represents an explicit application of Heidegger's tyrannophilic inclinations, adapted to an ethnocentric framework for post-Soviet Russia. On a broader level, Dugin positions Traditionalism as a counter to liberal postmodern deconstructionism. In *The Fourth Political Theory*, he claims a legacy rooted in covenantal bonds and sacred space, grounded in Traditionalism. For Dugin (2009, 194), "Muslims and Christians, Russians and Chinese, Hindus and Jews who challenge the present state of affairs, globalization, and American imperialism . . . are all virtually friends and allies."

At this point we enter into the connecting points between Dugin's existential stance and his geopolitics. More precisely, we deal with the connecting points between his antiliberalism and his defense of Russian Traditionalist imperialism rooted in the geopolitical concept of Eurasia. Based in Carl Schmitt, Dugin contrasts a theory of a multipolar world, which he praises, with what he (and conspiracy theorists worldwide) sees as the movement toward world government, led by disingenuous globalist elites. Finally, Dugin repeats and adapts Schmitt's claim that maritime powers should be resisted by continental ones. This is the connecting point between *The Fourth Political Theory* and the geopolitical strategy advanced by the idea of Eurasia.

As Leah Feldman (2023, 75) observes, Dugin frames neo-Eurasianism as a novel political epistemology designed for a post-Soviet, antiglobalist era. Andreas Umland (2007, 145) adds that the term "*neo-Eurasianism*" bears resemblance to the post-1968 European New Right, which introduced the notion of "ethnopluralism" – a euphemism that conceals a neoracist ideology.

This comparison reveals a key similarity between the two movements: Both use the language of cultural diversity to mask exclusionary and hierarchical views of identity, positioning themselves as defenders of multiple identities while advancing discriminatory and segregationist political goals.

However, it should be emphasized that while Dugin developed his idea of Eurasia through a wide range of intellectual and cultural influences, including aesthetic explorations of the occult (such as psychedelic mysticism), Western critical theory and neo-avant-garde performance art (Fenghi, 2020), his primary concern was Russia's cultural decline following the collapse of communism. He was deeply immersed in the 1920s intellectual debate between Westernizers and Slavophiles. The former believed that Russia was backward and that a revolution was needed to push Russia into a singular future. The latter believed that progress was pure illusion and Russia was endowed with a particular genius since the conversion of Kyiv to Christianity (Snyder, 2018, 84). The idea of Eurasia synthesized both trends. Eurasia was not just as a geopolitical framework but an essential cultural asset for Russia's revival. It provided a civilizational alternative to Western liberalism and globalism, positioning Russia as a counterbalance to the perceived moral and spiritual decay of the West.

The most significant influences shaping Dugin's conclusions on Eurasia came from linguist Nikolai Trubetzkoy, likely the first to develop the concept, as well as from geographer Lev Gumilev. Trubetzkoy's ideas on cultural diversity and his critiques of Western-centric universalism provided a foundation for Dugin's Eurasian vision, while Gumilev's theories on ethnogenesis and the unique characteristics of Eurasian civilizations added depth to Dugin's geopolitical and cultural framework.

Trubetzkoy envisioned a Eurasian polity formed through the cultural synergy of Turkic, Slavic, Mongol and other Asian-origin peoples, united against Western colonialism and Eurocentrism. Scholars like Vera Tolz and Susan Layton highlight significant parallels between Russian authors' and ethnographers' portrayals of Russian identity and Edward Said's postcolonial perspective. They suggest that certain Russian narratives, akin to Said's critiques, strive to reclaim cultural autonomy from Western-dominated frameworks of identity and historical interpretation (Tolz, 2008). Indeed Russia's marginality from Europe implied that "a Russian could not believe in the alterity of the Orient as readily and invariably as a European might" (Layton, 1994, 75).

Russia's engagement in the Caucasus exemplifies how Russian identity has historically been interwoven with the diverse perspectives of its Muslim communities. As Feldman (2012, 162) points out, the contributions of Muslim intellectuals from regions like Crimea, the Volga, the North Caucasus, Azerbaijan and Central Asia have been vital in shaping discussions around

Russian history and national identity. Dugin in particular sees these Muslim regions as integral to a cohesive Russian imperial identity. Rather than perceiving them as mere peripheries, he considers these areas essential to the cultural and geopolitical strength of the empire, reinforcing his vision of Russia as a multiethnic, civilizational force.

The second prominent intellectual influencing Dugin was Lev Gumilev, who spent thirteen years in Soviet prisons and forced labor camps and sparked the Eurasian revival in the 1980s with his theory of ethnogenesis, which puts all the blame for the failures of Russia on the West and the Jews. According to this concept, an ethnic group could, under the influence of a charismatic leader, develop into a "super-ethnos" (Burbank, 2022). Drawing on both Trubezkoy and Gumilev, Dugin develops his primary theoretical concern, which is the idea that each country "has its own structure that defines the elements of which it consists, and which gives them meaning and coherence" (Dugin, 2014, 6).

Dugin's Eurasianism is in the first place a program for government of the Eurasian Great Space centered on Moscow. At the international politics level, thus, Eurasianism holds that the world divides organically into four or five ethnocultural spheres, or "Great Spaces," each of which ought to be run according to its own values, or "particular and incommensurable horizon of being," by a powerful central administration (Hull, 2022, 132). Although as noted, Dugin is not the first and not even the most important scholar on geopolitics, his book *Basic Principles of Geopolitics* has helped transform the science of geopolitics in Russia from a discipline of fascist concern during communist times to its acceptance as a formal and recognized science (Mathyl, 2004, 188). Geopolitics is thus a science of ruling, a secularized product of sacral geography (Dugin, 1999, 2017, 14; Parland, 2005, 120).

Dugin envisions a world dominated by regional superpowers, with Russia positioned to exert influence over the territory of the former Soviet Union. Although he dismisses "communist ideology," he does not reject the "Soviet experience." In Dugin's view, the Soviet era positively expanded Russian power in the twentieth century and, crucially, its collectivist structure shielded Russia from what he perceives as the Western ailment of individualism. This collectivism preserved the rural, semifeudal character of the Eurasian people, a cultural essence he values deeply. Thus, behind Stalin, Dugin sees the shadow of Ivan the Terrible, symbolizing a return to traditional authoritarian roots (Laurelle, 2008, 142).

Dugin holds that the Soviet Union never conquered independent states such as Ukraine, Kazakhstan or Azerbaijan, since the latter were only administrative units. Moreover, Russia's takeover of the Crimea was a logical outcome of this thought.

However, even more than a geopolitical instrument, Eurasianism is a doctrine that proposes that every *ethnos* has its own tradition. It views the *ethnos* in the plural, without trying to establish any kind of a hierarchical system. In that sense, it is clear that Dugin's regional imperialism differs from liberal world imperialism.

As Tamir Bar-On correctly remarks, "If we think of imperialist anti-imperialism as a category, imperialist positions become a mechanism used to consolidate a supposedly anti-imperialist international project" (Bar-On and Paradela Lopez, 2023, 111). That is exacty what Dugin had in mind. Eurosianism is the key concept for an international "anti imperialist imperialist" enterprise. "Eurasianism, in itself, is gnoseological plurality. The unitary episteme of modernity – including science, politics, culture and anthropology – is opposed by the multiplicity of epistemes, built on the foundations of each existing civilisation – the Eurasianist episteme for Russian civilisation, the Chinese for the Chinese, the Islamic for Islam, the Indian for the Indian, and so on" (Dugin 2012, 99).

Dugin's *ethnorelativism*, however, is not restricted to moral and political values, but applies to concepts, theories and methods in general. He indeed is totally critical of the Western universal truth (Hull, 2022, 138). The liberal mind talks of truth and fake truth. For Dugin, instead there is a Russian truth and an American truth and both enjoy the same value. For Dugin (2014a, 6), this spirit of civilizationary differentiation thus should be applied to the fields of history, geopolitics, sociology, international relations, cultural studies, political science and so on. In any of these fields, the uniqueness of Russian civilization in comparison with all others, Western as well as Eastern, should be affirmed and defended.

In sum, more than a matter of geography, the concept of Eurasia for Dugin represents a philosophical approach. Eurasia represents geopolitics against globalization. While the latter represents the axis of cooperation of Europe, the United States and Canada, all of them positing the value of individuality and the market economy, Eurasia stands for the conservative philosophy of land-locked continentalism, namely the values of hierarchical structure, law, order and tradition.

It is of no doubt that there is a radical difference between Dugin's Traditionalism and de Benoist's. However, de Benoist and the New Right praise Dugin, because "unlike mainstream nationalists and the Slavophiles, [he] looks at the Soviet legacy as the continuation of the imperial idea in another form" (Camus, 2015, 86).

As de Benoist remarks, Dugin's idea of empire as opposed to the Western idea of nation-states has prompted him to stress that empire is always a multicultural space (Versluis, 2014, 85.) De Benoist thus applauds Dugin's culturalism and the principle of identity, which applies to all peoples alike. For Dugin, traditional Islam is threatened not only by liberalism, but also by the spread of "Wahhabism," which is paired with American global liberalism in preaching universal principles. It is the Sunni Muslim world that has sold out to "Atlanticist" powers. Muslim fundamentalism was indeed financed by the West in its fight against the Soviet Union (Laurelle 2007)/ As against Wahhabism on the one hand and liberal colonialism on the other, Dugin proposes an association of traditional Islam and Eurasia, namely a possible "strategic Russo-Muslim partnership," especially with Shiite Iran.

Dugin strongly asserts that religion is fundamentally "social, public, and even political" (Feldman, 2023, 83). Building on this view, he calls for a "popular front of traditional people [*front commun des gens traditionnels*]," uniting members of "religious societies," especially Muslims and Christians. This perspective informs his engagement with political Islam, as seen in his commentary on the Gaza conflict and his broader reflections on the emerging global order. In an article published at the Russian state-owned domestic news agency RIA Novosti, where Dugin discusses the ongoing war in Gaza, he claims that the Palestinian–Israeli conflict has "directly affected" all Muslims of the world, and this is the moment to build a new Islamic "pole" that could counter, along with other such "poles" – Russia and China – the unipolar world order led by the United States. After all, this is a struggle between the multipolar world and the unipolar world (Dugin, 2023).

He continues by being more specific on Israel and the Palestinians, and on a new world order that he expects will come even at the cost of a world war.

> Now the West, along with its Israeli proxy, is attacking the Islamic world, subjecting Palestinian Arabs to genocide. So, Islam's moment is coming. And in this potential war between Muslims and Western hegemony, which could erupt at any minute (as far as the Israelis are concerned, there is no doubt that they do not intend to stop until they have completely destroyed the Palestinians), the Islamic world has objective allies. In this situation [these allies] are, first of all, Russia and China, which itself is about to solve the problem of Taiwan. However, evidently, other front lines will gradually open. Could this lead to a World War III? Most likely, yes. (Dugin, 2023)

Furthermore, in the past few years, the degree of adoption of left-wing postcolonial perspectives is clearer than ever. Dugin also uses the language of "colonization" and "decolonization"; he also makes more frequent appeals to justice in the epistemic domain, arguing now for a "redistribution of the system of values" to "recognize the full-scale dignity of non-Western political thought" (Dugin, 2021, 73–74).

However, it remains to be seen whether representatives of classical national conservatism such as Putin or the French radical Right will endorse the philosophical strategy of Dugin. Indeed, several members of the French radical Right, including some associates of de Benoist, are critical of both Dugin's and de Benoist's approaches.

Gillaume Faye and Pierre Vial, for example, who make up the Bloc identitaire, think that Eurasia is not what Western Europe needs. This is precisely because Eurasia includes Muslims, who, according to Faye, have no right whatsoever to a say in the future of Europe. In the same vein, Faye (2010, 36) has criticized de Benoist's "ethnocultural relativism" because it implies a masochistic type of cultural equality. As Faye (2016, 104) deridingly remarked, "it seems that for de Benoist the right of alien nations ... in Europe ... is as important as that of the peoples of Europe." It is certainly Faye, and not de Benoist, who came to see Muslim immigration and Islam as the threat (Sedgwick, 2019, xviii). As against Eurasia, Faye and the *identitaires* propose the idea of Euro-Siberia, a white Europe that would include only the portion of Russia inhabited primarily by white people. For the Bloc identitaire, the main political goal is first and foremost to fight the Islamization of Europe.

It is not strange thus that, differently from Dugin, right-wing populist parties in Europe have shown support for Israel. Marine Le Pen even participated in the "hundred thousand march" against anti-Semitism that took place in Paris. For Marine Le Pen, the march constituted an opportunity to transfer the anti-Semitic label from her party to leftists and Muslim immigrants composing the pro-Palestinian camp. Geert Wilders in the Netherlands not only wants to ban Islamic schools, the Qur'an and mosques so as to halt the Islamization of the country, but his support for Israel is almost unconditional (Spektorowski, 2024, 16). Furthermore, from a different perspective, the question is whether Putin's Russian nationalism fits Dugin's imperial ideas, whether as posited by *Foreign Affairs*, Dugin represents Putin's brain or, on the contrary, he is far from Putin's old-style nationalism (Barbashin and Thoburn, 2014).

As early as 2013, Putin – very much in line with Dugin – declared that Eurasia was a major geopolitical zone expressing Russia's genetic code and needed to be defended from Western liberalism (Valdai, 2013). Putin has also brought most of the former Soviet republics into the Eurasian Economic Union. Under the Collective Security Treaty Organization, Russia keeps military bases in Armenia and Kyrgyzstan. Russian military bases can be seen in Abkhazia and South Ossetia, secessionist regions of Georgia. Like Dugin, Putin has drawn on a sense of ancient tradition, which leads him to invoke the role of Kyiv ("the mother of Russian cities") in the founding of the Russian nation in the ninth century (Berman, 2022). For Dugin, Russian cultural renaissance is integrally related to military intervention in eastern Ukraine, which he regularly calls Novorossiya (New Russia), a concept fully adopted by Putin. At the end of the 1990s Dugin was already saying that Ukrainian sovereignty presented a "huge danger to all of Eurasia." Total military and political control of the whole north coast of the Black Sea was an "absolute imperative" of Russian geopolitics

(Burbank, 2022). Finally the connecting points between geopolitics and philosophy become clear. "In essence the explicit purpose of Russia's war in Ukraine is the destruction of the West as a universalist project. According to Dugin, 'the West have abandoned traditional European culture ... and only Russia represents civilization" (Millerman, 2015).

It is not surprising that on a global scale, Dugin also expressed ambivalences toward Donald Trump. He even suggested that with Trump as the American president, the old Russian anti-Americanism was over. Despite being a billionaire, Trump embodies the "real" America, a heroic insurgency against the "globalist" beltway elites (Sharpe, 2017). Dugin envisions a new global architecture shaped by figures like Trump and Putin, yet he maintains a degree of caution regarding Trump. He questions Trump's commitment to a multipolar world order, expressing concern that, despite Trump's apparent alignment with Putin on Ukraine, he may unconditionally support Israel's actions against Palestinians. Dugin asks, "What role does Donald Trump's position play in this growing confrontation between the West and Islam?" He observes that while Trump is a "classic nationalist" primarily focused on American state interests rather than global domination, he is also, in Dugin's view, heavily influenced by the Zionist lobby within the United States. Consequently, Dugin suggests, "Trump will pursue a rather tough policy towards Muslims and especially Palestinians – perhaps even tougher than Biden" (Dugin, 2023).

Dugin's stance on Putin reveals a nuanced understanding: While he acknowledges that Putin does not aim to export Russia's authoritarian model to other nations, Dugin asserts that Russia faces an existential choice – to establish its own unique civilization or risk dissolution (Wright, 2022). Dugin's perspective finds alignment with de Benoist, who views the Ukraine crisis as evidence of a deeper ideological clash – one between advocates for a multipolar world and defenders of liberal capitalism as the global status quo (Tillet, 2017).

Together, Dugin's intellectual framework and Putin's political approach aim to reframe the conservative revolution, suggesting it is not simply a matter of authoritarianism versus democracy. Instead, they strive to validate alternative models of democracy, emphasizing a pluralism of values and governance structures distinct from Western liberalism. This approach positions the conservative revolution as a force that seeks to legitimize varied interpretations of democratic governance while opposing what they perceive as a universalizing, hegemonic liberal ideology.

The political implications of Dugin and de Benoist's intellectual efforts soon materialized, notably through China and Russia's response to President Biden's call for a virtual Summit for Democracy, which did not include China and Russia. In a joint statement, China depicted itself as a "high-functioning form of democracy," while Russia framed itself as a "democratic federative law-governed state," positioning both as alternatives to the perceived dysfunctions of the US system (Xinhuanet, 2021). This narrative serves a distinct purpose: to challenge the Western monopoly on defining democracy. For both powers, it is an assertion that democracy is not a uniform model dictated by Western ideals but a flexible concept adaptable to cultural and historical specificities. The West missionary role exporting universal values is rejected. This trait, according to Mr. Xi, is particularly alien to Asia, a continent that respects diversity and a "true multilateralism" guided by the UN Charter. A "shared future" is another way of saying "development first" – that is, rejecting any order guided by shared, universal values (Rennie, 2022).

The question of Dugin's alignment with the European New Right raises complex issues. While Dugin welcomes de Benoist's support, he is quick to underscore fundamental differences that go beyond stylistic nuances. He argues that, unlike their European counterparts, Russians are prepared for war. As Dugin puts it, "If the European New Right chooses us [Russians], that means it chooses the barbarian element, and therefore it must choose our methods of (violent) action" (Clowes, 2011, 43).

This assertion highlights a critical divergence: Where the New Right in Europe might focus on cultural and intellectual opposition, Dugin emphasizes the necessity of direct, often violent action to revive and protect civilization. Dugin's call to action is deeply linked to his radical interpretation of Heidegger, suggesting that it is Russia – not Germany – that is destined to revive and restore Western tradition (Love and Meng, 2017, 307). He envisions this mission as one that may require violent means, a stance underscored by the ongoing conflict in Ukraine, which, in his view, exemplifies the struggle to assert a Russian-led, tradition-based world order against Western liberal hegemony.

3.3 Bannon: Political Incorrectness and Traditionalism as Resistance to Liberal Hegemonic Discourse

Steve Bannon did not emerge in isolation. While he may not be placed within the same intellectual lineage as de Benoist and Dugin, his significance as a disseminator of ideas and his fusion of ideological synthesis with a combative person cannot be overlooked. Though no longer part of Trump's inner circle, his early contributions to the Trump phenomenon remain undeniable.

Bannon is Irish Catholic, hailing from a blue-collar background, and studied at Virginia Tech. He has experience working at Goldman Sachs and attempted a career in Hollywood, albeit unsuccessfully. It could be argued that his disdain for the image of the globalized world stems from his own inability to penetrate it. However, he still did very well as a political entrepreneur and consultant. As both chairman for Trump's campaign and onetime chief strategist for his White House, Bannon cultivated a reputation for a kind of vulgar brilliance – the erudition of an intellectual matched with the instincts of, in his words, a "street fighter." For some journalists, he is simply a provocateur, skilled at manipulating and exploiting prejudice – hence his success with Breitbart (Bouie, 2017)

According to Jeffrey Alexander (2017), the adult Bannon is indeed a person dominated by the sense of constant war. "Every day, we put up: America is at war, We're at war." This furious fighting-from-behind mentality certainly makes of Bannon an ideological leader of the contemporary American right. The reason for the war mentality is the conviction that, now more than ever, American liberalism is unstoppable. The social, cultural and sexual revolution is in full progress, and despite achieving political power, conservatives could not stop the march of progress expressed in the "the steady march of social incorporation, from industrial workers in the 1930s and Jews in the 1950s, to blacks, and the wide variety of ethnic communities, and non-conforming sexualities in the long 20th century" (Alexander, 2017).

Adding to this is a growing sense of frustration on the international stage, where conservatives see a steady decline in American global influence, especially in light of China's rapid ascent. Coupled with the forces of globalization and the transformation of the United States into a postindustrial economy that increasingly prioritizes education over unskilled labor, conservatives find themselves confronted by what seems like the perfect storm.

This provided an ideal platform for a debate among conservative ideologues and intellectuals concerning the future role of conservative thought and politics in the United States. One of the most intriguing debates among conservatives occurred between followers of Leo Strauss on the West Coast and their East Coast counterparts. This debate transcended the traditional divide between liberals and Republicans and has indirectly influenced Bannon's ideological evolution.

It is a noteworthy confrontation, particularly when we consider that Strauss, who became a significant ideological influencer in the conservative camp, was not a political man. He had dedicated much of his life to a careful analysis of classical works, ranging from Plato to Maimonides, Machiavelli and Hobbes. However, drawing precisely on the ideas of Strauss, these two competing intellectual factions – one led by Harry Jaffa and the other by Allan Bloom – debated the foundational philosophical influences of America. Jaffa, the leader of the West Coast Straussians, argued that America is rooted in ancient philosophy, while Bloom, the leader of the East Coast Straussians, contended that its foundations lie in the works of early modern philosophers such as Thomas Hobbes and John Locke.

In political terms, the question focused on whether America's survival depends on the virtue of the people, as West Coast Straussians believe, or on the maintenance of constitutional norms, as East Coast Straussians believe (Heer, 2016). The intellectual divide also significantly relates to the United States' role in global politics. Neoconservative figures of the East Coast such as Nicholas Kristol and Paul Wolfowitz believe in the mission of America as a beacon of democracy for the world. They categorically reject Trump's leadership style for America. Kristol's publication, *The Weekly Standard*, for example, serves as a prominent platform for opposing Trump's populist approach.

West Coast Straussians sharply diverge from that perspective. Intellectuals such as Charles Kesler and Angelo Codevilla view the current era as one filled with revolutionary potential. They see Trump as a pivotal figure capable of instigating significant regime change. Kesler, who is a professor of government at Claremont McKenna College and the editor of the *Claremont Review of Books*, was clear in stressing that America nowadays may be facing "the Weimar problem." For him, the liberal elites have deteriorated American national culture. They have destroyed the virtues necessary to sustain republican government. If you live in the Weimar Republic, Kesler implicitly argues, a figure like Trump could come as a relief (Heer, 2016).

Codevilla, a retired professor of international relations, follows this line of thought. America, for Codevilla, has already suffered a revolutionary regimental change. It is precisely the American elite who destroyed what was great about the country. The logical conclusion is that America is in need of a counterrevolution.

Serious publications like *The American Mind* of the Claremont Institute, *First Things* and *The American* have actively expressed and elaborated upon these ideas. The Claremont Institute, for example, promotes a continuation of the political liberalism that the US Constitution embodies. In contrast, national conservatives and Integralists aim to establish a pan-Christian confessional state, seeking to prohibit abortion, gay marriage and similar practices.

This perspective has found political expression in the Heritage Foundation, which since 2022 has emerged as a pivotal think tank for national conservatism. Drawing inspiration from Viktor Orbán's brand of Christian nationalism in Hungary, the Heritage Foundation has focused its efforts on dismantling what it perceives as the American deep state. Significantly, since 2023, it has forged a cooperative relationship with Hungary's state-funded Danube Institute Project, further solidifying its commitment to these ideological pursuits.

There is no doubt that the American alt-right and Bannon himself have gravitated toward the Heritage Foundation. Indeed, Bannon has championed Project 2025, organized by the Heritage Foundation, which aims to map out specific strategies for using the federal government to punish critics and opponents. Furthermore, the Christian nationalism promoted by the Heritage Foundation has fueled the alt-right's belief that America should be a purely Anglo-Saxon country.

Indeed, the main foe of the alt-right appears to be the American Constitution. "American constitutionalism and exceptionalism won't rescue European Americans from multiculturalism and finally from replacement" (Morgan, 2017). Here, the bankruptcy of American exceptionalism based on free markets is the point to stress. The terminus of this line of thinking was explicitly stated by Jared Taylor, the editor of *American Renaissance*, in his "Open Letter to Cuckservastives" (a contemptuous term for old-style American conservatives). Accusing these conservatives of defending "principles," Taylor demands a shift. Things "that you love about America ... are not rooted in principles, but ... are rooted in certain people, namely white people" (Taylor, 2015).

The extent to which the American alt-right draws inspiration from the French New Right's strategic use of intellectual discourse and media to influence cultural and political narratives is a significant question. There is no doubt that the alt-right's famous phrase "You [Jews, Muslims, Latinos] will not replace us" has its origins in the writing of the popular Renaud Camus (Williams, 2017). Moreover, de Benoist's *Manifesto for a European Renaissance* was an important text shaping the political views for members of the alt-right such as Richard Spencer and Jared Taylor, as well as Steve Bannon, with whom de Benoist maintains contact. As John Morgan writes, one of the common features of the alt-right and the New Right is that both considered that the Nazi and fascist past experiences are not relevant for current times. Those "who want to refight the Second World War are soundly rejected by both [alt-right and New Right]" (Morgan, 2017). Yet, while both the alt-right and the New Right might reject the label of "fascism," both actively fight against the theoretical hegemony of liberalism. As Milo Yiannopoulos puts it: "A specter is haunting the dinner parties, fundraisers and think-tanks of the Establishment: the specter of the 'alternative right' that is here to stay as political contenders in most Western democracies" (Yiannopoulos and Bokhari, 2016).

Despite commonalities, however, de Benoist's perspective notably diverges from the American alt-right regarding the issue of race. De Benoist frames his struggle as a defense of "all identities in the world" against the forces of global homogenization, which he sees as eroding distinct cultural and national identities. In stark contrast, the American alt-right places a significant emphasis on white identity, viewing the preservation of the white race as central to its ideological battles.

Thomas Main concludes, "the alt-right is a form of radical Gnosticism as fundamental in its rejection of the American democratic tradition as the

Communist Party line of the 1930s" (Main, 2018, 7). But while communists aspired to overcome that tradition-first set of values with economic and political revolution, Taylor envisions a racist response.

Still the open question is to what extent is Bannon entrenched in this political current, and to what extent is his endorsement tactical? It is clear to most members of the alt-right, such as Richard Spencer, that Bannon is not necessarily one of them, but a fellow traveler contributing to the cause. Both Bannon and the alt-right have the same enemy, the liberal pro-multicultural elites of Washington, and both are clearly critical of the global economic elites. However, for some scholars, they differ on the identity question. Bannon is a civic rather than an ethnic nationalist (Main, 2018, 213). Still, his civism is accompanied and filtered by a deep antiliberalism and by a great respect for ethnonational traditionalism. Moreover, Bannon most of all was affiliated with the Traditionalist movement and is considered an admirer of Evola's political thought (Teitelbaum, 2020).

He was introduced to Evola's thought by William Strauss and Neil Howe's *The Fourth Turning*, which depicts history in cycles of cataclysmic and order-obliterating change. Critics of Bannon point out that Evola was a pagan and Bannon a Catholic, defending the obscure idea of Judeo-Christian values against Islam. However, Evola's followers were both pagan and religious, substantiating Evola's claim that the forces of history are led by two factions: "history's demolition squad," enslaved by blind faith in the future, and those whose "watchword is *Tradition*" (Evola, 2002, 129). It is difficult not to see Bannon's apocalyptical view of politics in the Western world other than through Evola's lens. That is why most of the American alt-right ideologues consider Bannon the gate through which Evola's ideas of a hierarchical society, run by a spiritually superior caste, can be recovered during a period of crisis (Beiner, 2018, 11).

Bannon himself believes that Trump is the unconscious instrument of this necessary clash with what remains of the Enlightenment. Bannon indeed sees in Trump's leadership the continuation of the populist spirit, which with or without Trump should lead to institutional transformation, namely to an end of liberal institutions.

Bannon emphasizes the differences between Trump of 2016 and Trump of the Conservative Political Action Conference in March 2023, shortly before the first of his indictments. In 2016, Trump told his constituency, "I am your voice." In 2023, he said, "I am your warrior. I am your justice. And for those who have been betrayed, I am your retribution" (Homans, 2024).

Bannon is delighted about this revanchist state of mind, which aligns with his emphasis on the potency and allure of political incorrectness, while reveling in the utilization of Carl Schmitt's formula of "us against them." In 2013, when

Bannon was turning Breitbart into the far Right's dominant media outlet, he presented himself first and foremost as a Leninist of the Right, a supporter of economic nationalism. He attempted to challenge the most conservative members of the Republican Party and American society with a direct and shockingly non-politically correct approach. It did not stop there, however. As the keynote speaker before an audience of the French National Front, Bannon exposed a central cultural tenet of fascism: "Let them call you racists, let them call you xenophobes ... Let them call you nativists. Wear it as a badge of honor" (Smith, 2020, 65). By employing racist rhetoric and economic nationalist arguments, he aimed to evoke antiestablishment sentiments.

Bannon understands that politics is a fight between clearly bounded identity groups. As Shery Berman (2018) remarked, appeals and threats to group identity will benefit Republicans more than Democrats. That is the reason Bannon stresses that he couldn't "get enough" of the Left's "race–identity politics." "The longer they talk about identity politics, I got 'em ... I want them to talk about race and identity ... every day."

In short, as a political strategist, Bannon recognizes the power of challenging political correctness and engaging in what he sees as culture wars to fuel populist movements. Furthermore, Bannon understands that the Left has inadvertently provided conservatives with new weapons to pursue their censoriousness.

To be precise, the use of identity politics in American politics is not a recent phenomenon. Its roots can be traced back to earlier periods, including its utilization by the Democratic Party during the Civil War era in 1864, as well as its manifestation in the insurgent campaigns of Strom Thurmond and George Wallace during the 1960s. However, the impact of identity politics in contemporary times is notably amplified by "the grotesque online culture wars [that] fuel populism" (Nagel, 2018, 15).

In 2016, the resurgence of identity politics took on a more crude and reactionary form, emerging as a countercultural response to the prevailing ideological landscape dominated by left-leaning social interpretations of diversity and assertions of cultural rights for minorities. This resurgence occurred amidst a growing backlash against globalization and immigration. The prevailing narrative posits that globalization and immigration are championed by an alliance of rational liberal economists and multiculturalist social liberals. Central to this narrative is the notion of a repressed white identity, which is portrayed as being invaded and marginalized by the forces of globalization, fueling sentiments of resentment and disillusionment among certain segments of the population.

Up to this point, Bannon aligns closely with the perspectives of figures like de Benoist. However, a point of departure arises about the role of violence and political incorrectness and regarding which identities should lead the charge of rebellion. While de Benoist tries to clean up fascism of its violent connotations, or to "[make] white supremacy respectable again," Bannon goes the opposite way.

By any normative understanding, "racist," "xenophobe" and "nativist" are *negative* words from both a moral and rational point of view. Bannon, however, understands the moment, urges followers to drop the façade and recommends the promotion of irrational moves as virtuous. In this point he is clearly closer to Dugin's approach.

However, while both Dugin and Bannon advocate for a more assertive defense of traditional values and national sovereignty, their views on Islam diverge significantly. Dugin sees potential common ground with certain elements within Islam in the broader struggle against liberalism, whereas Bannon views Islam as a fundamental threat to Western civilization. Bannon claims that the Judeo-Christian West (meaning the antithesis of Islam) is at the early stages of a global war against Islamic fascism, and the West has to organize against it as against liberal globalization.

As can be discerned, for Bannon, both resistance efforts against Islamic and liberal globalization require an international perspective. Endowed with organizational acumen, Bannon has dedicated significant efforts to rallying the "International" of the populist right. He envisions the realization of a dream: the formation of a global antiglobalist alliance (*The Economist*, 2024, 17).

Always inspired by Traditionalism, Bannon and a small group of right-wing power brokers have been planning political mobilizations on a global scale. In secret meetings organized in hotel suites and private apartments in Washington, DC, Europe and South America, they conspire to revolutionize the world order and reorganize geopolitics on the basis of archaic values rather than modern ideals of democracy (Teitelbaum, 2020).

He envisions that populist forces share a common view of how nonliberal international institutions should look. One of the institutions that should be dismantled and changed is the European Union, which he views as emblematic of globalization. He demands European populist leaders abandon it.

However, Bannon faces a partial disappointment from his right-wing allies. His efforts to dismantle the European Union have faced silent resistance from his right-wing allies such as Viktor Orbán or Giorgia Meloni. Despite their shared aspirations to reform the European Union into a more closed, nationalistic and less liberal entity, they hardly strive to abandon it. This setback does not deter Bannon from continuing his conspiratorial enterprise. Following that line of thought, he reflects the new-old tendencies of the American political right: the embrace of autocrats rather than the defense of democracy.

If in the past, American conservatives rejected Russia's undemocratic regime, they nowadays see Russia as the bulwark of conservatism – a mirror for the right-wing worldview. Richard Spencer, for example, has referred to Russia as "the sole white power in the world." Bannon adds something that is especially shocking to liberal ears: "We did not serve in the Marine Corps to go and fight Vladimir Putin because he didn't believe in transgender rights." He hailed Mr. Putin as "anti-woke" just hours before Russia's assault on Ukraine, and he clearly let him know which side of the cultural war in America he is on (Tamkin, 2022).

The American political Right now expects what Dugin and de Benoist had already forecasted. If postwar Europe created political systems that varied from country to country but were still "built everywhere on principles of law, human rights and personal freedom," the new conservative revolution has established the internationalization of illiberalism, where the national rights of Western identities are portrayed as the new-old resistance to global "human rights" cultural colonialism.

This is not a return to a preferable form of liberalism as advocated by certain conservatives. Instead, it signifies a "postliberal order" that repudiates liberal values such as religious liberty and pluralism and notably relinquishes a defensive stance (Deneen, 2021).

Still the question is whether there are differences between the European and the American New Right. Scholars such as Mihai Varga and Aron Buzogány distinguish between the European New Right, which is anti-American, and the American and Eastern European New Right, which advocates conservative nationalism (Varga and Buzogány, 2021, 5–6). In truth, however, the French New Right does not inherently espouse anti-American or anti-Eastern European sentiments. Instead, it portrays entities such as Trump's America, Putin's Russia and the broader national conservative movements in Eastern Europe as complementary figures in the fight against globalization.

However, as noted, Bannon's emphasis on religion as salvation, contrasting with secularism as the root of societal decay, slightly defies the pagan criteria of the French New Right. When Bannon speaks of defending Western civilization, he predominantly refers to the defense of Christian civilization. In some instances, he incorporates the concept of Judeo-Christian civilization, despite the fact that Jews may not always be considered part of the national mainstream in certain contexts.

Finally, while this criteria would not be accepted by de Benoist and Dugin, what puts Bannon close to Dugin is his spirit of conflict and total war and the conviction that we are in a time of decisions. Indeed, both Bannon and Dugin harbor a conviction that we are currently in war times, signaling a belief in the urgency and gravity of the present moment. In a manner reminiscent of Dugin, Bannon presents in his 2010 documentary *Generation Zero* his interpretation of how history unfolds. According to Bannon, the first phase is the Unraveling, during which the traditional work ethic is replaced by a culture centered around money. This period marks the elevation of the self to a godlike status. *Generation Zero* presents a stark assessment of the current crisis, suggesting that it will ultimately determine the success or failure of the American experiment. Bannon concludes that it is imperative for the Right to emerge victorious in order to establish a new foundational moment for America.

Similar to the West Coast Straussians, he warns that if the Left prevails, the American dream will be lost. The documentary is revolutionary in its call to action, suggesting that the unfolding of the new world requires a violent and apocalyptic confrontation as a first step. Bannon is indeed a conservative revolutionary who synthesizes motives from both the Left and Right. It is noteworthy that he praised the American Weathermen, militant Maoists who sought to instigate the violent overthrow of capitalism in the 1960s (Alexander, 2017).

Finally, as noted, despite that both Bannon and Dugin understand that we are arriving at a time of definitions and that means violence, the differences between the two are indeed stark, particularly in their respective views on the composition of the coalition of resistance against liberalism and left-wing progressives.

Despite sharing with Dugin Traditionalist values, Bannon does not include Islam in his alliance of resistance to liberalism. These divergences underscore the complexities within the New Right. In short, while they all oppose progressive liberalism, they diverge significantly, particularly in defining who comprises the spiritual "anti-materialist bloc" and who should be excluded despite its antiliberalism. It is of no doubt that from his *War Room* podcast he will continue to promote a permanent right-wing conservative revolution, which has already left a lasting imprint on Trump's discourse and resonates more than ever nowadays within populist right-wing movements globally.

Paradoxically, the next great struggle Bannon will face is likely to unfold within the MAGA movement itself. Trump's alliance with a high-tech aristocracy – including figures like Elon Musk, podcaster David Sacks and crypto exchange founder Tyler Winklevoss – marks one of the most unexpected alliances in American political history. In this dynamic, the tech industry emerges as an alternative power center challenging the traditional Republican establishment.

Despite sharing nationalist and reactionary views with Bannon, these figures have become the target of his self-declared war on what he calls technological feudalism. As Bannon argues, "We haven't created anything on the technology side like the airplane or the internal combustion engine or the steam engine or anything big. It's all been algorithms" (Pogue, 2025). This internal MAGA conflict will likely shape future ideological battles between reactionary populists who embrace global technocratic innovations and those who remain committed to Traditionalist frameworks.

3.4 Latin America: The Brazilian New Right? Olavo de Carvalho

Probably the name of Olavo de Carvalho would not have been heard at a global level if not for what observers claimed to be his philosophical and clear political influences on the right-wing populist president Jair Bolsonaro. When on October 28, 2018, Bolsonaro held his first live stream after his electoral victory, among the four books he had in his desk was Carvalho's bestseller of 2013, *The Minimum You Need to Know Not to Be an Idiot*.

Carvalho was already known by that time in Brazil as a conflictive self-made Brazilian intellectual, with no rich academic background, but who became popular because of the aforementioned bestseller and the previous *O Imbecil Coletivo* (*The Collective Imbecile*) (1996), which has already reached its eighth edition.

With a background of journalism in the 1970s, Carvalho started in the 1980s writing books on cultural criticism and political philosophy such as *Aristóteles em Nova Perspectiva* (*Aristotle in New Perspective*), *Machiavelo, A Confusão Demoníaca* (*Machiavelli, or The Demonic Confusion*) and others. At the same time, Carvalho embarked on teaching independent, nonacademic courses centered on topics that reflected his personal interests throughout his life, including comparative religions, political gnosticism, revolutionary mentality, astrological symbolism and traditional metaphysics. Undoubtedly, these subjects diverged significantly from the focus of the academic intellectual landscape in Brazilian universities. Moreover, Carvalho's emergence as a prominent rightwing esoteric philosopher posed a challenge for the Brazilian academic community. His prominence evoked memories of the significant influence wielded by Catholic Integralists in Brazilian politics during the 1930s and 1940s, a legacy that some found difficult to reconcile with the contemporary intellectual milieu.

At the methodological level, what was also striking was Carvalho's success in establishing a confrontational, semitotalitarian discourse in the public sphere. As George Wink claims, much more than an intellectual method, Carvalho has created a system that efficiently shields his ideology and makes his arguments irrefutable (Wink, 2021, 197).

His more direct aim was the delegitimization of the left-wing establishment within intellectual circles, especially by denouncing what he saw as a communist cultural revolution dominating Brazil. For Carvalho, the egalitarian Marxist cultural project, for example, survived the death of political communism. It manifested itself in modern expressions such as the São Paulo Forum, which he characterizes as a criminal organization. Essentially, Carvalho sees the continuation of the egalitarian postcommunist dream through Gramsci's organic intellectuals, whose task is to achieve cultural hegemony through a gradual and subtle series of psychological mutations over time.

The Gramsci-inspired Western globalist project, according to Carvalho, has this very task: to shift the people's traditional mode of thought or their common sense into a revolutionary one. That is why there is a clear attempt to destroy religion through sexual freedom and transformation, freedom to choose whether one is woman or man, etcetera. This is a second reality that challenges the sense of proportions and the nature of things.

In a broader sense, it could be argued that Carvalho echoed a new Brazilian spirit characterized by an affinity for issues associated with Rightism, including moral conservatism, religiosity and the free market. In order to promote this worldview, there is a need to destroy what is left from Marxism. This context created fertile ground for a conservative discourse to gain intellectual and political traction, facilitating social receptivity to Carvahlo's political messages and contributing to the success of Bolsonaro. Indeed, his rhetoric has played a significant role in bolstering the campaign of Bolsonaro. As a strategic populist polemic whose lifeblood is sarcasm, humor, and verbal violence his work was successful (Wink, 2021, 211).

However, the question lingers about his right-wing conservative precedents in Brazilian political history. The history of the rise of the Right in Brazil had been related directly to moral questions. Indeed, due to their broad social appeal, moral issues have been politically mobilized at various key moments in Brazilian political history. The first instance was marked by the rise of Integralism in the 1930s, the second by the military coup of 1964 and the third by the social and economic crisis that preceded Bolsonaro's ascent to power. Bolsonaro's statement "Let us unite the people, cherish the family, respect religions and our Judeo-Christian tradition, combat gender ideology while preserving our values" (Iamamoto, Kubík, and Summa 2023, 785) encapsulates the essence of Brazil's moral revolution throughout its history. There is no doubt that Carvalho was deeply influenced by the roots of Brazil conservative ideology. For scholars such as Arthur Hussne (2020), Olavismo precisely continues the tradition of Brazilian Integralism. Scholars such as George Wink agree with Hussne and suggest that Carvalho and the Integralist leader, Plínio Salgado, have much in common.

Whether Brazilian Integralism, led by the Ação Integralista Brasileira (AIB), qualifies as a fascist movement has been a focal point of scholarly debate.

António Costa Pinto argues that the AIB was the most successful fascism-inspired movement in Latin America, emphasizing its adoption of fascist organizational methods and its appeal to nationalist and authoritarian sentiments (Costa Pinto, 1994, 143). This view aligns with Tucci Carneiro's observation that the authoritarian ideology in Brazil during the 1930s and 1940s was influenced significantly by Italian Fascism and German National Socialism (Carneiro, 1999, 12). However, Helgio Trindade offers a more nuanced perspective, acknowledging the AIB's fascist characteristics, including its rigid structure, performative rituals and nationalist discourse, yet highlighting its unique ideological framework. Trindade (1979, 4, 289) suggests that, despite these fascist attributes, the AIB's foundations were deeply rooted in a religious morality more akin to Portuguese Salazarianism, with its emphasis on traditionalism, Catholicism and corporatism rather than the more revolutionary, secular nationalism found in Italian Fascism.

Indeed, for several scholars, the Integralism of Salgado was a conservative movement "guided by a traditional family model," where men were seen as breadwinners and responsible for the moral direction of the family (Ferreira, 2016). The state was envisioned as a union of all families, a concept encapsulated in the slogan "God, Fatherland, and Family."

Thus, despite fascist influences, Salgado should not be labelled a full-fledged *fascist* (Wink, 2021, 183). Moreover, despite the fact that observers in those years portrayed the AIB (1932–1938) as a "foreign phenomenon inherently opposed to the Brazilian spirit," in reality, the movement's values resonated widely and were largely accepted within Brazilian society, particularly in the 1930s (Victor, 2005, 19–20; Pinheiro Ramos, 2014, 334).

The remaining question is in what sense Carvalho continues along this ideological line. Carvalho, best categorized as a conservative Catholic, felt a strong calling to guide Brazilians away from what he viewed as the enslavement of modernism. His outlook aligns closely with an ultramontane Catholic reaction against the various modern attempts to relativize Catholic doctrine – encompassing opposition to Protestantism, rationalism and communism.

Carvahlo thus advocated the restoration of the primordial order of tradition and promoted a societal regeneration through the restoration of the integrity of faith in human existence (Wink, 2023). Central to Carvalho's views is a fundamental rejection of the values and principles of the Enlightenment. Relying on Eric Voegelin's (1901–1985) theological perspective in his *The New Science of Politics*, Carvalho considers that the Gnosticism and heretical messianism expressed in utopian ideas of progress have led the Western world to an humanitarian crisis. Heretical messianism, according to Carvahlo, takes the form of progressivism, positivism, Marxism, communism and even fascism and National Socialism, which were Satanic regimes accountable for destroying the real word of God (Carvalho, [1995] 2015, 2001) The question, however, is to analyze how the world of modernity should be opposed.

As such, Olavismo aligns well with the Traditionalist rebellion and with the metapolitical intellectual enterprise of de Benoist, Dugin and Bannon. However, while Dugin and Bannon contend that we are approaching an hour of definitions, interpreted as nearing a phase of fascist violent activism, Carvalho subscribes to a different type of metacultural and social activity.

Carvalho's brand of Traditionalism emphasizes the role of Christian communities, both Catholic and Protestant, in a global spiritual revival. He envisions these communities, particularly those in Africa and Asia, playing a pivotal role in re-Christianizing Europe and North America – regions that were once the source of Christianization for much of the world. According to Carvalho, these Christian groups, now rooted in the Global South, retain the true spiritual vitality that Europe and the West have lost. In his view, the moral and spiritual strength of these communities could serve as a counterbalance to the secularism and moral decline of the West, leading a heroic effort to restore Christian values in the very regions that had first spread them to the world.

Of especial importance in explaining Olavo's entrance into the Traditionalist world is his first contact with Michel Veber (1926–2003), who founded the first real Traditionalist group in Brazil, the Academia Kan-Non, which combined Traditionalist doctrine with the Chinese martial arts practices of T'ai chi ch'üan (Tàijí quá). In 1980, Carvalho, then a freelance journalist and writer on astrology, invited Veber to lecture on Guénon and Traditionalisma at his Escola Júpiter (Jupiter School) in São Paulo. He was very impressed by Veber and described him as "my professor," with whom he discussed Guénon's personal connection to authentic Hindu and Islamic esoteric teachings.

It did not take much time and Carvalho published his first known Traditionalist article "Morality without God?" which advances the Traditionalist conception of the "perennial philosophy" as a road to resolve problems of cultural relativism that stem from the diversity of human social and ethical practice (Sedgwick, 2021, 164). Carvalho was convinced that esoterism should be at the center of Traditionalist studies, and in his philosophical search, he led his growing number of followers to become part of an esoteric Sufi organization called Tradição (Tradition). Later on, he supported another organization, the Maryamiyya, where he got in contact with Martin Lings (Abu Bakr Siraj al-Din, 1902–2005), the leading follower of Schuon in England and a Muslim and follower of Guénon himself. From Lings, he learned that in order to enter the Maryamiyya (unlike Sufi orders in the Muslim world, the Maryamiyya was a secret organization) there is a need to "enter Islam". Following that direction, Carvalho and many of his followers "entered" Islam and even delivered lectures on Islamic Traditionalism, recommending Sufism and Sufi masters as capable of orienting religious people who came from other traditions. With the passing of years, however, Carvalho himself denied or softened the Traditionalist and Sufist influences in his political thought.

Indeed, while initially influenced by Traditionalist convictions advocating for the adoption of "Oriental doctrines" such as Islam as the only alternative to barbarism, Carvalho eventually abandoned this viewpoint, leading to tension with his admired Schuon. Carvalho's engagement with Neo-Thomism, especially through the influence of Stanislavs Ladusāns, illustrates his approach to reconciling traditional Catholic metaphysics with the challenges of modernity. Ladusāns, as a Neo-Thomist, sought to create a dialogue between Thomistic philosophy and contemporary human sciences. Carvalho built upon this by asserting that modernity's ills could be addressed through a return to transcendent truth grounded in Catholic doctrine. For Carvalho, philosophy was the path to a universal truth, which, in his view, stood in opposition to the relativism and ideological distortions of modernity. Truth for Carvalho is not relative, and in order to be able to see reality, the individual consciousness must be "kept clean," without ideological filters (Bruno, 2019, 5). In his *A Nova Era e a Revolução Cultural* (*The New Age and the Cultural Revolution*) (Carvalho, 2014, 93), Carvalho states the importance of the independence of individual thought, and he understood that human beings live in the in-between area. The role of philosophy, however, is to lead to truth, which is God's truth. That is what Voegelin defined as *Ordnungswissen* (knowledge of the sublime order).

The battle between the Christ and the Antichrist is a real-world battle and should be won by Christ. Indeed, Carvalho's perspective suggests that the philosophical pursuit of unity of knowledge and consciousness leads ultimately to Christ. He draws parallels between this pursuit and the efforts of Catholics to maintain a state of grace despite the presence of sin. In both cases, individuals strive to remain in an illuminated state of existence, seeking spiritual enlightenment and alignment with divine truths. This highlights philosophical inquiry as a means to attain illumination and spiritual fulfillment, akin to the pursuit of grace in Catholic doctrine. As noted, this way of thought leading to transcendent, meta-materialistic view of the world, history, and politics, was not uncommon to religiously influenced thinkers, such Eric Voegelin (Bruno, 2019, 6–7).

Carvalho's stance in his later years illustrates an interesting pivot: While he acknowledged the perceived moral void left by secularism, he ultimately rejected the path of Islamization for the West. This departure is notable, especially given Carvalho's previous alignment with certain Traditionalist thinkers, such as Guénon, who endorsed Islam as a return to spiritual values.

Instead, Carvalho criticized the impulse among some Traditionalists to adopt Islam, positioning himself in opposition to what he viewed as a misguided solution to Western moral and cultural decay. This shift highlights his broader aim to address the spiritual crisis of the West without turning to non-Christian religious frameworks.

Carvahlo stressed that "any intelligent Christian, Catholic or not, can take advantage of René Guénon's teachings without joining the Guénonian project," so long as they know what that project is (Carvahlo, 2016). It is at this point that Carvalho becomes a classic right-wing thinker. He had precedents in Latin American history. Some of the intellectuals and ideologues who preceded him were from the Argentinean national catholic brand, during the early and mid twentieth century.

Novelist Leopoldo Marechal (1900–1970) was well versed in Guénon's work on esotericism and symbolism, drawing from it in his literary explorations. Reactionary figures like priest Julio Meinvielle (1905–1973) similarly endorsed Guénon's critique of modernity, while Alberto Ezcurra Medrano (1937–1993), founder of the fascist Tacuara movement, emphasized Traditionalism's "radical critique of the modern world" (Sedgwick, 2022)

Carvalho, like some of these figures, expressed sentiments that have been widely criticized as anti-Semitic. His foundational beliefs were shaped by the notion that a syndicate of Jewish bankers held control over global affairs – a view rooted in anti-Semitic tropes. This perspective, common among certain conspiracy theories, aligns with broader elements of Traditionalist and reactionary thought that emphasize hidden elites shaping the world order.

However, it's noteworthy that his stance toward Jews and Israel shifted amidst the ongoing confrontation between the West and Islam, as well as the rising anti-Semitism evolving from left-wing postcolonialist sources. He recognized that Muslims and their leftist enablers, rather than Jews, were the perceived problem. This change in perspective represents a significant ideological shift akin to an "ideological somersault."

Carvalho criticizes the idea propagated by anti-Semitists that Jews wield control over global media. He argues that if Jewish entities would have held substantial influence over the press, mainstream media would exhibit consistent and overt support for Israel, even to the detriment of other nations. However, Carvalho observes the opposite is happening. Israel is often criticized and attacked by the world press. Conversely, he perceives that the cultural war waged by Muslims in the West is portrayed with "innocent and moving images" (Carvalho, 2010), while in reality it is a barbaric war.

It is not strange, therefore, that Carvalho would emphasize Israel's pivotal role in the ideological struggle that would influence the course of the Western world. His analyses underscored the significance of Israel as a focal point for understanding broader geopolitical dynamics and ideological conflicts shaping global politics.

The debate between Carvalho and Dugin, titled "The USA and the New World Order: A Debate between Olavo de Carvalho and Aleksandr Dugin" (Carvalho and Dugin, 2011), highlights not only the divergent perspectives regarding Israel, but also their differences regarding the role of violence and the place of the United States in the wide right-wing ideological spectrum. Carvalho begins the debate by asserting that at the level of basic convictions there are no differences between him and Dugin, therefore apparently there is nothing to debate about.

> Does he believe in God? So do I. Does he think a metaphysics of the absolute is possible? So do I. Does he wager that life has a meaning? So do I. Does he understand traditions, homeland, and family as the values that must be preserved above supposed economic and administrative conveniences? So do I. Does he see with horror the globalist project of the Rockefellers and Soros? So do I. Therefore at first sight it is not possible to organize a debate between two people who are in agreement. (Carvalho and Dugin, 2011, 5)

However, immediately afterward, Carvalho stresses the wide gap separating a philosopher as he defines himself and a political activist as he defines Dugin. "To say that Professor Dugin is at the center and pinnacle of power is a simple matter of realism. To implement his plans, he has at his disposal Vladimir Putin's strong arm, the armies of Russia and China and every terrorist organization of the Middle East, not to mention practically every leftist, fascist and neo-Nazi movement which today operate under the banner of his 'Eurasian' project" (Dugin and Carvalho, 2011, 6). Indeed, Carvahlo's characterization of Dugin's line of thought as that of a "right-wing Bolshevik" or "leftist traditionalism" reflects the complexity and perhaps ambiguity of Dugin's ideology.

According to Carvalho, we have nowadays three projects of global dominance, which he tentatively calls the "Russian-Chinese," the "Western" (sometimes mistakenly called "Anglo-American") and the "Islamic" projects. The agents that personify these projects today are as follows: (1) the ruling elite of Russia and China, and particularly the secret services of these two countries; (2) the Western financial elite, as represented by the Bilderberg Club, the Council on Foreign Relations and the Trilateral Commission; (3) The Muslim Brotherhood, the religious leaders of several Islamic countries and the governments of some Muslim countries.

Of these three agents, Carvalho (2011, 7) claims that "only the first can be conceived of in strictly geopolitical terms, since its plans and actions correspond to well-defined national and regional interests. The second, which is more advanced in the implementation of its plans for world government, places itself explicitly above any national interests ... and in the third project, the conflicts of interests between national governments and ... a Universal Caliphate are always ultimately resolved in favor of the latter."

Carvalho ultimately concludes that the conception of global power pursued by different ideological agents is inherently incompatible. While he resists multiple geopolitical projects, his strongest disdain is reserved for Dugin's revolutionary geopolitical agenda. Though Carvalho may agree with Dugin on the diagnosis of the West's spiritual decay and detachment from traditional values, he sharply diverges when it comes to the strategic paths proposed for addressing the materialist world. Carvalho rejects Dugin's geopolitical ambitions, viewing them as fundamentally at odds with his own vision for restoring moral and cultural order, which is deeply rooted in Christian metaphysics rather than revolutionary or Eurasianist frameworks

Moreover, while Dugin believes that the strong Eastern tradition has a sacred right to take the world back from its Western exile, Carvahlo believes in the recovery of the West through Midwestern rural traditions and its priests. Carvalho stresses the fact that Dugin does not understand the "real America." One face of America is the managerial, liberal, Manhattan politically correct world. The other face is Traditionalist America, where a traditional Catholic movement that wants the Tridentine Mass back and rejects the modernization of the Catholic Church is flourishing together with a fervent American Evangelical Protestant community.

In this sense, Carvalho rejects the New Right's attempt to associate Western globalism with the United States. The West, according to Carvalho, should be defined beyond its liberal institutions. In his mind, America's "metacapitalism" project could be overcome in a similar manner to how the socialist project of the Soviet Union was overcome.

In short, while Dugin considers that there is only one United States, which represents the peak of Western civilization based in human rights, the promotion of democracy and free market economics (Carvalho and Dugin, 2011, 18), for Carvalho, there is also a Traditional, real America that constitutes a pole of resistance. Moreover, notably, Carvalho places Traditional America, the Jewish nation and traditional Jews on equal footing. In his perspective, all of them are threatened by the Western globalist project. This point is remarkable; Carvalho also notes that Judaism is threatened by secular Jews, and that there is a duty of Christians to protect them, or at least to save them from extinction when they are threatened (Caravalho and Dugin, 2011).

Finally, Carvalho aims to dismantle Dugin's ideological framework by asserting that the globalist elite is not an enemy of Russia, China or Islamic countries. Instead, Carvalho posits that the global elites are collaborators with these nations in an effort to undermine the political, military and economic power of the United States (Carvalho and Dugin, 2011, 14). The "destruction of American power will remove the last reasonable hurdle to the establishment of a world government. Then, all that will be left, is the sharing of the spoils among the three globalist schemes, the Western, the Russian-Chinese and the Islamic one" (Carvalho and Dugin, 2011, 14).

In short, while Dugin emphasizes the cultural and spiritual heritage of Eurasia as an alternative to the materialism and decadence of the West, Carvalho looks to rural traditions, particularly those found in the American Midwest (Teitelbaum, 2021). While Dugin, similar to de Benoist, finds "a lot of very charming (Eurasian) features in the South and Central American societies" and includes Shiite Islam in the coalition of resistance, Carvalho defends the West as a whole, and America's conservative establishment in particular (Carvalho and Dugin, 2011, 27–28). In more senses than one, Carvalho and Dugin represent the contrasting poles of the reaction against woke liberal culture and supranational organizations.

In current times, as a result of wars in Gaza and Ukraine, two different coalitions within the conservative revolution confront each other. One "coalition of resistance" as proposed by Dugin seeks to defeat both Ukraine and Israel. In contrast, we could guess that Carvalho, if still alive, would support Israel. He would probably prefer, however, that the liberal coalition that supports Ukraine and Israel would become an ideological home for white Christian identitarianism and a proud Jewish state. Carvalho would certainly embrace Carl Schmitt's conclusions in his *Glossarium* of June 1950: "Poor those Jews that don't want to be Zionists" (Rosler, 2023).

One could argue that Carvalho's iteration of the postcolonial right is arguably characterized by anti-Semitic sentiments, albeit it maintains a pro-Zionist stance. Conversely, Dugin's fascist variant exhibits both anti-Semitic and anti-Zionist tendencies. Absolutely, the ideological battle lines drawn by Carvalho and Dugin illustrate the complex and sometimes contradictory nature of the global struggle against liberalism. Similarly to the debate between de Benoist and Faye regarding the complementary roles of de Benoist's cultural pluralism and Faye's exclusionist nationalism, here we also have two versions of who composes the antiglobalization camp.

The final question is to what extent Bolsonaro's presidency embodies Carvalho's political philosophy in practice (Bruno, 2019, 4). At a strictly political level, Carvalho found himself as a political influencer in the new government that shook Brazil and the world. Carvalho was tempted to accept the post of minister of education but he refused. Instead he actively recommended individuals for key government positions who shared his conservative and Traditionalist views. By promoting figures like Ricardo Vélez Rodríguez and Ernesto Araújo, who were aligned with his ideological stance and expressed admiration for thinkers like Guénon and Evola, Carvalho aimed to shape Brazil's political landscape according to his worldview. Araujo in particular shared with Carvalho the same interests in Traditionalism, expressed quite clearly in his article "Trump and the West," in which he praised Bannon and also recommended to the public readings such as Guénon's *Crisis of the Modern World* and Evola's *Metaphysics of War* (Araújo, 2017, 356). What is certain is that Carvahlo's growing influence garnered attention even from publications such as the Council of the Americas' *The Americas Quarterly*, which published an interview with him (Winter, 2018).

Of no doubt, Bolsonaro's skepticism toward globalism, his stance against what he and his supporters term "cultural Marxism," and his defense of family values and opposition to abortion, gay rights and secularism in public education echoes Carvalho. Moreover, Bolsonaro, was not only associated with Carvalho but also with Bannon, and the political scientist Filipe Martins (currently a counselor to the Brazilian president on international relations) – all of whom see Israel as a model of successful nationalism and all of whom indirectly hint that Trump and the American conservative camp together with Israel should be forerunners of a right-wing association against the progressive camp.

Both Dugin and de Benoist are critical of this stance. Despite the fact that Bolsonaro is a nativist, he is scorned by de Benoist. Indeed, de Benoist's nativism contrasts with Bolsonaro's white nativism in Brazil, as well as with Zionist nativism in the Middle East, because the latter are not considered nativism, but colonialism. De Benoist also criticizes Bolsonaro's foreign policy decisions, particularly because he prioritize alliances with Israel and Saudi Arabia while adopting a hostile stance toward China and Russia (De Benoist, 2019). In short, we can conclude that the different coalitions of resistance against liberalism are far from assuming a common stance.

Nonetheless, we must stress that still both conflicting currents share the perception that the traditional model of liberal governance is no longer viable or desirable. Both currents propose an alternative to liberal democracy, which they often frame as being more authentic than national or cultural identities. Both are illiberal in nature, and both emphasize identity (whether ethnic, national or cultural) over universal values. Most of all, as Carl Schmitt did, they devise a multipolar world as against liberal governance.

4 Conclusions: Fascism in the Making? From Metapolitics to Political Praxis

A wide-ranging debate has developed in recent years among scholars increasingly worried by the weakness of liberal democracy and the growing electoral power of national populist movements in Europe. Scholars such as Yascha Mounk (*The People vs. Democracy*, 2018), Steven Levitsky and Daniel Zimblatt (*How Democracies Die*, 2018) and Patrick Deneen (*Why Liberalism Failed*, 2018), among others, have either pointed to the inherent tension between liberalism and democracy or emphasized the loss of shared norms in liberal democracies as leading to the end of democracy.

What seems to be clear to those scholars is that contemporary democracies are more likely to decay gradually than to die quickly (Berman, 2021, 72). This Element endeavors to demonstrate that the crisis of liberal democratic representation coincides with the gradual but consistent development of an ideological alternative. Once the diffusion of political ideas helped foster democratic transitions. Today it facilitates democratic backsliding (Diamond, 2024). This shift underscores the increasing political significance of the ideological frameworks advanced by intellectuals, as these ideas shape and bolster populist rhetoric and action. Through the analysis of the ideological encounters and differences between Alain de Benoist, Alexander Dugin, Steve Bannon and Olavo de Carvalho, this Element seeks to elucidate this alternative.

As this Element emphasizes, through their differences and agreements they challenge from a perspective of the Right what appears to be a petrified cultural consensus on race, identity and colonialism. While most texts that explore the emergence of the national populist Right or the ideology of the alt-right emphasize its authoritarianism, racial supremacism and rejection of other cultures, this Element presents a contrasting portrayal.

This emerging form of "differentialist" right-wing ideology represents a departure from traditional racist supremacy, instead embracing an intellectual lineage rooted in fascist theory that promotes ethnonationalist self-determination. Referred to as a "fascism of resistance," it stands against global liberalism, proposing a world order where autonomous, conservative ethnonational communities flourish, both within Western societies and beyond. This vision offers an alternative to the liberal global model, which it frames as a form of modern colonialism while simultaneously positioning itself as a counterpoint to leftist postcolonial critiques.

In contrast to the inclusive strategy of left-wing postcolonialism, which seeks to address liberalism's exclusions through a broadened, integrative framework, the emerging postcolonialism on the Right advocates a form of "pluralist exclusionism." This ideological shift calls for a conservative revolution that aims to redefine democratic principles around the "rights of peoples," emphasizing the prerogative of communities to maintain distinct, even exclusionary, cultural and ethnic identities. Under this view, local and national entities assert their sovereignty by establishing the right to "discriminate" within their own borders, essentially embodying a "my home, my rules" approach, while encouraging other regions and cultures to follow suit in their respective domains. Indeed against conservative nostalgia or liberal domination, they propose a domestic and international order centered around a return to the "ethnos" (Drollet and Williams, 2018), and around the idea of national spheres of influence.

Whereas progressives highlight the grievances of the colonized "Third World" against the white man, the new fascism of resistance places the grievances of the whites of the United States, Europe and the dismantled Russian eastern empire on equal footing with repressed non-Western identities. Indeed, unlike white supremacists, this new fascism of resistance presents the protection of traditionalist white Americans (Smith and King, 2021, 460), as complementary to the thesis of cultural protection of other world cultural identities.

Indeed, the New Right that stands as the basis of this fascism of resistance proposes an international, multilevel illiberalism aligning radicalisms – white and black, Right and Left – as travel partners against global liberalism. In short, they propose a postcolonialism of the Right in which black racism and white racism stand together as brothers in arms.

The question, however, is whether this development could be defined as fascist, post-fascist, or simply a renewal of the old conservative revolution for postmodern times. This Element takes note of James Gregor, Tamir Bar-On, Kurt Weyland and others who object to the facile and incorrect usage of the term *fascist*. Nonetheless, despite criticism, this Element considers the new domestic developments in Western societies and the shifting world international order from liberal unilateralism to multilateralism as the perfect framework for the reception of the New Right's postcolonial conservative revolution. This implies the expansion of a fascist worldview, defined as fascism of resistance including the Global North and the Global South.

My argument thus is that liberal society is not merely facing an irrational, nationalist, anti-intellectual populism that insists on "only one legitimate viewpoint, that of the dominant nation (Stanley, 2019, 36; Traverso, 2019). Nor is it solely contending with fascist falsehoods, which undoubtedly form a core part of the fascist doctrine and influence the rise of "fake truth" in contemporary discourse (Finchelstein, 2022). The current reaction against liberalism, however, transcends a simple regressive or revanchist stance that would be inherently inferior to liberalism's rational claims to truth. Instead, it reflects a deeper challenge, suggesting that liberalism's purported universality and rationality are themselves subjects of dispute and critique.

Paradoxically, the influence of these challenging ideas is more pronounced than ever, even in shaping the ideological evolution of an ostensibly "non-ideological," opportunistic and anti-intellectual figure like the newly reelected president Donald Trump. A significant debate has emerged in the United States over whether Trump's recent rhetoric, particularly since 2020, edges closer to fascist tendencies, diverging notably from his 2016 approach.

The evolution in Trump's rhetoric might appear to some as mere populist opportunism or rhetorical flourish, crafted to resonate with a polarized electorate. Yet, as this analysis points out, there are indicators that suggest a deeper ideological substratum underpinning this discourse. Dugin understood very clearly what Trump's victory meant. "The victory of Donald Trump ... marks the beginning of a fundamental shift in the world order. It is a global conservative revolution" (Dugin, 2024).

It is of no doubt that Trump echoes the writings of the Heritage Foundation and Bannon's philosophy of praxis even without understanding its meaning. Nowadays, the practical face of Bannon's philosophy of praxis is continued by the America First Policy Institute, a right-wing think tank that became Trump campaign's primary partner in making concrete plans for Trumps return to power. Like Project 2025, the institute developed a plan for setting the policy agenda and for staffing every federal agency with Trump partisans and for shaping the strategies to advance America's conservative revolution.

This is not merely an attempt to attribute a generally accepted moral vocabulary to questionable social behavior (Göpffarth, 2020, 252). I would even argue that they have reintroduce the value of serious ideological debate into the forefront of Western societies. As Matt Grossmann and David Hopkins have observed regarding the political clash in the United States, "Republican partisans tend to view political conflict as fundamentally ideological in nature, while Democrats perceive it as a clash of competing group interests" (Grossman and Hopkins, 2015, 123).

The claim that the Right is becoming theoretically innovative while liberalism has become technocratic and legalistic since the triumph over communism is indeed a provocative one, but it contains elements of truth that are worth exploring. The final speculative question thus is how threatening and challenging for liberals this intellectual development is.

Writing in 2019, Jennifer Lind and William Wohlforth (2019, 77) observed that current illiberal states are not foreseen as endorsing imperialist policies, and there is hardly a danger of totalitarianism in sight. However, since Russia's invasion of Ukraine, this view is logically scrutinized. Nowadays, with wars in Eastern Europe and the Middle East already raging, and ties between revisionist states becoming more pronounced, we cannot dismiss the tragic option that interrelated regional struggles overwhelm the international system and create a crisis of global security unlike anything since 1945 (Brands, 2024). Even without considering the option of war, still, as Angela Merkel already pointed out, we are already seeing a new thinking in terms of national spheres of influence, in which principles of international law and human rights are being brought into question (Pfister, 2019). Despite difference of interests, China, Russia and a postliberal United States could certainly in theory and practice strive for Carl Schmitt's world order built around spheres of influence.

While regarding Western Europe, thinking critically, we might harbor doubts about de Benoist's assumption that a new postliberal European identity could emerge at a regional level, still de Benoist exclusionary ethnopluralism has become one of the most important ideological developments in the discourse of the Right. The idea that European ethnic regions suffered from the same cultural colonialism as Global South identities is innovative thinking gaining track not only in right-wing ideological circles. Empirical studies suggest the potential for a populist eruption in, for example, the Basque country and Catalonia, in Nord Pas de Calais and in the Greek Islands is greater than in their respective national counterparts (Van Hauwaert and Schimpf Dandoy, 2019, 307). Yet, while this last observation many raise hopes in de Benoist and Piccone, still Europe's regional identities are deeply embedded within the structures of the European Union and its liberal democratic norms.

Differently from Western Europe, Dugin's vision of a Eurasian bloc centered around Russia is much more challenging to Western liberalism. For several observers, the war in Ukraine's final outcome will be achieved by one result: that the age of liberal American-led globalization is over and Russia's war as a cleansing act of violence "does not represent only a return to the traditional fascist battleground, but also a return to traditional fascist language and practice" (Snyder, 2022b). Indeed, the sense of Russia's national decay and call for palingenesis is difficult to ignore. Furthermore, far from being rejected, Russian imperialism seems to be accepted by a great part of the Global South. Indeed, across a vast span of countries stretching from continental Eurasia to the north and west of Africa, we find societies that have moved closer to China and Russia over the course of the past decade. The result, as a report of the Bennet Institute for Public Policy (2022, 1) stresses, is that the world is torn between two opposing clusters: a maritime alliance of democracies led by the United States, and a Eurasian bloc of illiberal or autocratic states centered upon Russia and China. Nowadays however, we may cast doubts about this conclusion. Rather than a maritime alliance of democracies against autocracies, we might soon find, if we follow America's development under Trump, a Western alliance of illiberal democracies against established autocratic states.

We are witnessing a somehow similar scenario through the alliances springing up and debates raging around the war in Gaza. While support for Israel is increasingly dwindling among Western democratic nations, it is noteworthy that the conflict in Gaza has sparked internal debates among the new conservative revolutionaries. Populist politicians such as Marine Le Pen, Jair Bolsonaro, and the British hard-line former home secretary Suella Braverman have publicly rejected left-wing anti-Semitism, with Dutch politician Geert Wilders clearly expressing his support for Israel. In contrast, figures like Putin, along with intellectuals such as Aleksandr Dugin and Alain de Benoist, have made their opposition to Israel evident. As we have seen, Olavo de Carvalho seriously and innovatively considered the role of Israel and the United States – particularly the role of an identitarian America and an identitarian Jewish Israel – within the context of an antiliberal coalition.

At first glance, the differences regarding the conflict in Gaza or regarding the role of American power may wrongly lead to the assumption that the contradictions and debates within right-wing national conservative politicians and intellectuals forging a global alliance against liberalism turn that alliance into something incoherent and harmless. However, it is far from that and there are reasons to worry.

Historical examples help us understand how, despite differences, currents of thought became hegemonic or challenging. The First and Second International could be portrayed as assemblies of disperse left-wing associations that collapsed. Yet they helped propagate communist and social democratic ideologies. Also, fascists worldwide had disagreements. In 1934, Italian fascists tried to organize an universal theory of fascism in Montreaux Switzerland. The attempt had mixed fortunes (especially concerning resistance to the chosen ideological platform of "Roman universality," which was more amenable to Mediterranean "Latin" countries than their central and northern European counterparts). The delegates at Montreaux disagreed on almost everything. They debated and disagreed upon questions of race, the so-called Jewish question, the role of Christianity and the balance between national independence and international collaboration. Indeed the transnational history of fascism was not a matter of "successful" diffusion of a core ideology from a supposed center outward. Instead it was coproduced by diverse political strategies through interactions and frictions, through a kaleidoscope of creative translations and, in the end, through trial and error (Kallis, 2021, 213).

Hence we should not only expect disagreements among parties, movements and intellectuals of this New Right's revolutionary umbrella. The ongoing debate, contradictions and tensions among prominent representatives of the New Right illustrate the progression of the conservative revolution through discourse.

In summary, by examining the intellectual frameworks of these four New Right intellectuals, this Element underscores the urgent need for liberals in the Western world to not only engage in self-reflection but also to confront an alternative ideological narrative that is both perilous and coherent. In this regard, the new fascism of resistance today emerges as an ideological movement prioritizing the decolonization of the Western mind, with a focus on liberating it from its own constructs, particularly the ideology and practices of the Enlightenment.

This has been a highly under-theorized topic because of the focus placed on the rise of populism as a sociopolitical movement devoid of a thick ideological offering. This Element thus joins a new trend of studies that challenge the "thin ideological" thesis and easy interpretations of the "new" fascist uprising as a pure white supremacist dictatorial anti-intellectual movement. That loose perspective makes life much easier for liberals; however, it is far from realistic.

While providing a road map for a liberal resurrection is far from the scope of this Element, as Timothy Snyder (2022a) remarks, precisely in an era when moral universalism and liberal consensus have given way to the hard realities of moral relativism and postliberal political competition, the Ukrainian resistance could allow liberalism to once more become a fighting faith for renewal.

However, there is much more than that. Liberals indeed should take people's legitimate grievances seriously. Many Western citizens reject illegal migration, viewing it as a source of disorder and a drain on public resources. They are also anxious about losing their jobs to new technology while observing arrogant globalists prospering in society. However, for the "left behind," the actions of globalizers are a curse rather than a blessing. Finally, instead of ceding the power of national myths and symbols to political opportunists, liberals need to get over their embarrassment about patriotism, the natural love of one's country (*The Economist*, 2024, 9). The struggle against fascism of resistance unfolds through nationalism rather than universal liberalism or postcolonial progressivism.

References

Abrahamsen, Rita, Jean-François Drolet, Alexandra Gheciu, Karin Narita, Srdjan Vucetic and Michael Williams (2020) Confronting the international political sociology of the New Right. *International Political Sociology* 14(1) (March): 94–107.

Alexander, Jeffrey (2017) Raging against the Enlightenment: The ideology of Steven Bannon. Center for Cultural Sociology. Based on a lecture to the Yale Political Union (April 13).

Arato, Andrew (2013) Political theology and populism. *Social Research* 80(1) (Spring): 143–172.

Araújo, Ernesto (2017) Trump e o Occidente. *Cadernos de Política Exterior* 3(6) (December): 323–357.

Arendt, Hannah (1945) Imperialism, nationalism, chauvinism. *Review of Politics* 7(4): 441–463.

Bale, Jeffrey, and Tamir Bar-On (2022) *Fighting the Last War: Confusion, Partisanship, and Alarmism in the Literature on the Radical Right.* Lanham, MD: Lexington Books.

Bar-On, Tamir (2001) The ambiguities of the Nouvelle Droite 1968–1999. *European Legacy* 6(3): 333–351.

Bar-On, Tamir (2007) *Where Have All the Fascists Gone?* Aldershot: Ashgate.

Bar-On, Tamir (2008) From fascism to the Nouvelle Droite: The dream of pan-European empire. *Journal of Contemporary European Studies* 16(3): 327–345.

Bar-On, Tamir, and Paradela-López, Miguel (2023). Antiimperialismo y anticolonialismo de la derecha radical: Una propuesta de categorización. *Revista CIDOB d'Afers Internacionals* (132), 92–112. https://recyt.fecyt.es/index.php/cidob/article/view/97895.

Barbashin, Anton, and Hannah Thoburn (2014) Putin's brain: Alexander Dugin and the philosophy behind Putin's invasion of Crimea. *Foreign Affairs* 31: 1–6.

Bardeche, Maurice (1961) *Qu'est-ce que le fascisme?* Paris: Les Sept Couleurs.

Beiner, Ronald (2015) Russia's ecumenical jihadist: Who is Aleksandr Dugin and why is he saying all these terrible things about the West? *Inroads*, no. 37 (Summer–Fall): 491–506.

Beiner, Ronald (2018) *Dangerous Minds: Nietzsche, Heidegger and the Return of the Far Right*. Philadelphia: University of Pennsylvania Press.

Bennet Institute (2022) A world divided: Russia, China and the West. Written by Roberto S. Foa, Margot Mollat, Han Isha, Xavier Romero-Vidal, David Evans and Andrew J. Klassen. Bennet Institute for Public Policy. Center for the Future of Democracy. Cambridge University.

Berezin, Mabel (2011) The normalization of the Right in post-security Europe. Revised for Polity Press. Armin Schaefer and Wolfgang Streeck, eds. October 1. Prepared for *Democracy in Straightjackets: Politics in an Age of Permanent Austerity*, Schloss Ringberg (March 23–26).

Berman, Paul (2022) The intellectual catastrophe of Vladimir Putin. *Foreign Policy* 52 (March). https://foreignpolicy.com/2022/03/13/putin-russia-war-ukraine-rhetorichistory.

Berman, Shery (1998) *The Social Democratic Moment: Ideas and Politics in the Making of Interwar Europe*. Cambridge, MA: Harvard University Press.

Berman, Shery (2018) Why identity politics benefits the right more than the left. *The Guardian* (July).

Berman, Shery (2021) The causes of populism in the West. *Annual Review of Political Science*. polisci.annualreviews.org.

Bernhard, Patrick (2018) Fascist empire? Nazi Germany and the problem of colonialism. *Contemporanea* 21(1): 120–124.

Bhabha, Homi (1994) *The Location of Culture*. London: Routledge.

Bhambra, Gurminder K. (2014) Postcolonial and decolonial dialogues. *Postcolonial Studies* 17(2): 115–121.

Bickerton, Christopher J., and Carlo Invernizzi Accetti (2021) *Technopopulism: The New Logic of Democratic Politics*. Oxford: Oxford University Press.

Bittner, Joechen (2016) Is this the West's Weimar moment? *New York Times* (May 31).

Bloemraad, Irene, Will Kymlicka, Michèle Lamont and Leanne Son Hing (2019) Membership without social citizenship? Deservingness and redistribution as grounds for equality. *Daedalus* 148(3): 73–104.

Bluhdorn, Ingolfur, and Butzlaff, Felix (2018) Rethinking populism: Peak democracy, liquid identity and the performance of sovereignty. *European Journal of Social Theory* 22(2): 191–211.

Bogdandy, Armin von, and Adeel Hussain (2021) Carl Schmitt's international thought and the state. In Annabel Brett, Megan Donaldson and Martti Koskenniemi, eds. *History, Politics, Law: Thinking through the International*. Cambridge: Cambridge University Press, pp. 131–159.

Bouie, Jamelle (2017) Steve Bannon's intellectual reputation is a charade. *Slate* (September 12).

Brands, Hall (2024) The age of amorality. Can America save the liberal order through illiberal means? *Foreign Affairs* 103(2): 104–117.

Brown Rachel, Heather Hurlburt, and Alexandra Stark (2020) How the coronavirus sows civil conflict. *Foreign Affairs* (June 6). www.foreignaffairs.com/articles/world/2020-06-06/how-coronavirus-sows-civil-conflict.

Bruno, Victor (2019) Philosophy, mysticism, and world empires: Elements of the political philosophy of Olavo de Carvalho. *Political Science Reviewer* 43(1): 1–34.

Burbank, Jane (2022) The grand theory driving Putin to war. *New York Times* (March 22).

Burbank, Jane, and Frederick Cooper (2010) *Empires in World History: Power and the Politics of Difference*. Princeton, NJ: Princeton University Press.

Bures, Eliah (2020) Beachhead or refugium? The rise and dilemma of New Right counter culture. *Journal for the Study of Radicalism* 14(2) (Fall): 29–64.

Bülow, Marisa von, and Rebecca Neaera Abers (2022). Denialism and populism: Two sides of a coin in Jair Bolsonaro's Brazil. *Government and Opposition*, 1–19. https://doi.org/10.1017/gov.2022.14.

Camus, J. Yves (2015) A long-lasting friendship: Alexander Dugin and the French radical right. In Marlene Laruelle, ed. *Eurasianism and the European Far Right: Reshaping the Europe–Russia Relationship*. Lanham, MD: Lexington Books, pp. 79–96.

Camus, J. Yves (2019) Alain de Benoist and the New Right. In Mark Sedgwick, ed. *Key Thinkers of the Radical Right*. Oxford: Oxford University Press, pp. 73–90.

Camus, J. Yves, and Nicolas Labourg (2017) *Far Right Politics in Europe*. Cambridge, MA: Harvard University Press.

Camus, Renaud (2011) *Le Grand Remplacement*. Neuilly: Reinharc.

Carneiro, Maria Luiza Tucci (1999) Prefácio. In João Ricardo de Castro Calderia, ed. *Integralismo e política regional*. Sao Paulo: Annablume, pp. 11–14.

Carvalho, Olavo de (1997) *O Imbecil Coletivo*. Faculdade da cidade editora (4th edition). Rio de Janeiro: Faculdade da cidade editora.

Carvalho, Olavo de (2001) Gnósticos e revolucionários. *O Globo* (July 21).

Carvalho, Olavo de (2010) Israel ante o poder global. *Diário do Comércio* (June 8).

Carvalho, Olavo de (2013) *O Mínimo Que Você Precisa Saber para Não Ser um Idiota* (Record).

Carvalho, Olavo de (2014) *A Nova Era e a Revolução Cultural: Fritjof Capra & Antonio Gramsci* (4th edition). Campinas, Brazil: VIDE Editorial.

Carvalho, Olavo de (2015) Em pleno surto de deslumbramento pela escola tradicionalista de Guénon e Schuon. Facebook (January 24). www.facebook.com/carvalho.

Carvalho, Olavo de (2015 [1995]). *O Jardim das aflições: De Epicuro à ressurreição de César – ensaio sobre o materialismo e a religião civil.* Campinas: Vide.

Carvalho, Olavo de (2016) As garras da Esfinge – René Guénon e a islamização do Occidente. *Verbum* 1:1 and 2 (July and October). Republished on Olavo de Carvalho. http://olavodecarvalho.org/as-garras-da-esfinge-rene-guenon-e-a-islamizacao-do-ocidente.

Carvalho, Olavo de, and Aleksandr Dugin (2011) *The USA and the New World Order* (March 7). http://debateolavodugin.blogspot.com/2011/03.

Césaire, Aimé (2000) *Discourse on Colonialism*. Translated by Joan Pinkham (1950). New York: Monthly Review.

Clarkson, Stephen. (2004) Global governance and the semi-peripheral state: The WTO and NAFTA as Canada's external constitution. In Stephen Clarkson and Marjorie Cohen, eds., *Governing under Stress: Middle Powers and the Challenge of Globalization*. New York: Bloomsbury, pp. 153–173.

Clowes, Edith W. (2011) *Russia on the Edge: Imagined Geographies and Post-Soviet Identity*. Ithaca, NY: Cornell University Press.

Corradini, Enrico (1923) *Discorsi politici 1902–23*. Florence: Editorial Vallecchi.

Costa Pinto, António (1994) *Os Camisas Azuis: Ideologia, elites e movimentos fascistas em Portugal, 1914–1945*. Lisbon: Editorial Estampa.

Costa Pinto, António (2012) *The Nature of Fascism Revisited*. Boulder, CO: Social Science Monographs

Davidson, Miri (2024) On the concept of the pluriverse in Walter Mignolo and the European New Right. *Contemporary Political Theory*. https://doi.org/10.1057/s41296-024-00732-x.

De Benoist, Alain (1966) *Qu'est-ce que le nationalisme*. Doctrinaire text (un groupe de travail réuni autour de "Fabrice Laroche").

De Benoist, Alain (1979a) *Les Idées a `l'endroit*. Paris: Libres-Hallier.

De Benoist, Alain (1979b) *Vu de droite: Anthologie critique des idées contemporaines*. Paris: Copernic.

De Benoist, Alain (1981) *Comment peut-on être païen?* Paris: Albin Michel.

De Benoist, Alain (1990) Only the Indo-European traditional model could set politics above the economy. *Elements* 68: 32–36.

De Benoist, Alain (1991) L'imperialisme américaine. *L' Idiot International* 44. January 16.

De Benoist, Alain (1994a) The idea of empire. *Telos* 98–99: 95 (originally delivered as a lecture at GRECE's 24th National Congress, devoted to the topic "Nation and Empire." Paris, March 24, 1991).

De Benoist, Alain [Roberto de Harte] (1994b) Entre Jacobinisme et séparatisme. *Éléments* 12. http://grece-fr.com/?p=3733.

De Benoist, Alain (1994c) Three interviews with Alain de Benoist. *Telos* 98–9: 173–207.

De Benoist, Alain (1994d) *Le grain de sable: Jalons pour un fin de siecle*. Paris: La Labyrinthe.

De Benoist, Alain (1995) Democracy revisited. *Telos* 95: 65–75.

De Benoist, Alain (1996) Confronting globalization. *Telos* 2(108): 117–137.

De Benoist, Alain (1999) What is racism? *Telos* 114: 11–48.

De Benoist, Alain (2003) Julius Evola, réactionnaire radical et metaphysician engagé: Analyse critique de la pensée politique de Julius Evola. *Nouvelle École*, no. 53–54: 147–169.

De Benoist, Alain (2007) Preface. In *Cahiers du Cercle Proudhon* Paris: Avatar Editions.

De Benoist, Alain (2010) Junger & Drieu La Rochelle. *Counter Currents*, July 16. www.counter-currents.com/2010/07/junger-and-drieu-larochelle.

De Benoist, Alain (2011a) *Beyond Human Rights: Defending Freedoms*. London: Arktos.

De Benoist, Alain (2011b) 'L'immigration, armée de réserve du capital. *Eléments* 139 (April–June): 1–6.

De Benoist, Alain (2014) Identity and difference. *The Occidental Observer*: 1–7. Translator Lucian Tudor. September 13–14.

De Benoist, Alain (2019) Jair Bolsonaro's program is appalling. *Geopolitics* 26(1). www.geopolitika.ru/en/article/alain-de-benoist-jair-bolsonaros-program-appalling.

De Benoist, Alain (2021) Aucune élection, fût-elle présidentielle, ne peut créer les conditions de la veritable revolution dont notre people a besoin. [Interview] Breizh-info 27.10. www.breizh-info.com/2021/10/27/173367/de-benoist-alain-presidentielle-elections.

De Benoist Alain, and Charles Champetier (1999a) 2012 Manifesto of the French New Right in Year 2000. https://s3-eu-west-1.amazonaws.com/alaindebenoist/pdf/french_new_right.pdf.

De Benoist, Alain, and Charles Champetier (1999b) *2012 Manifesto for a European Renaissance*. London: Artkos.

Deneen, Patrick (2018) *Why Liberalism Failed*. New Haven, CT: Yale University Press.

Deneen, Patrick (2021) Abandoning defensive crouch conservatism. *The Post Liberal Order*, November 17.

Diamond, Larry (2024) How to end the democratic recession. *Foreign Affairs* 103(6): 126–140.

Drolet, Jean François, and Michael William (2018) Radical conservatism and global order: International theory and the new right, *International Theory* 10(3): 285–313.

Dugin, Aleksandr (1999) 2017 *Foundations of Geopolitics*, Kindle edition.

Dugin, Aleksandr (2009) 2012 *The Fourth Political Theory*. Translated by Mark Sleboda and Michael Millerman. London: Arktos.

Dugin, Aleksandr (2012) Lecture, "Traditionalism and Sociology/The Figure of the Radical Subject." Colloquium on Evola, Curitiba, Brazil, September.

Dugin, Aleksandr (2012) 2014 *Putin vs Putin: Vladimir Putin Viewed from the Right*. Edited and translated by John B. Morgan. London: Arktos.

Dugin, Aleksandr (2014a) *Eurasian Mission: An Introduction to Neo-Eurasianism*, ed. John B. Morgan. London: Arktos.

Dugin, Aleksandr (2014b) *Poslednii Blog*. Moscow: Akademicheskii Proekt.

Dugin, Aleksandr (2015) *Eurasian Idea and Postmodernism*. http://4pt.su/en/content/eurasian-idea-and-postmodernism. Cited in John Mosbey (2017) Aleksandr Dugin: Philosophical aspects of the fourth political theory. Draft working paper, p. 23. www.academia.edu/32437212/Aleksandr_Dugin_Philosophical_Aspects_of_the_Fourth_Political_Theory.

Dugin, Aleksandr (2021) *The Great Awakening vs the Great Reset*. London: Arktos.

Dugin, Aleksandr (2023) MEMRI. "Anti-liberal Russian philosopher Dugin: 'The time For the final battle has come." RIA Novosti, November 28. Ria.ru/20231112/konflikt-1908909297.html.

Dugin, Aleksandr (2024) Trump's victory: A global conservative revolution. *Arktos*. November 7. https://arktos.com/2024/11/07/trumps-victory-a-global-conservative-revolution.

Duranton Crabol, Anne Marie. (1988) *Visages de la NouvelleDroite. La GRECE et son histoire*. Paris: Presses de la Fondation Nationale des Sciences Politiques.

Eatwell, Roger (2000) The rebirth of the "extreme right" in Western Europe. *Parliamentary Affairs* 53(3): 407–425.

Eatwell, Roger (1996) On defining the "Fascist Minimum": The centrality of ideology. *Journal of Political* Ideologies 1(3): 303–319.

The Economist (2024) Nationalists of the world unite! February 17.

Evola, Julius (1986) Adapted from *Gliuomini e le rovine* [*Man and the Ruins*]. Rome: Giovanni Volpe,1972; 1st ed. 1953), cited in Griffin (1995) *Fascism*. Oxford: Oxford University Press.

Evola, Julius (1995) *Revolt against the Modern World*. Rochester, VT: Inner Traditions.

Evola, Julius (2002) *Men among the Ruins: Post-war Reflections of a Radical Traditionalist*. Inner Traditions.

Evola, Julius (2007) *The Metaphysics of War*. Inner Traditions.
Evola, Julius (2013) *Fascism Viewed from the Right*. Translated by E. Christian Kopff. London: Arktos.
Faivre, Antoine (1996) L'historien et le pérennialisme. *Politica Hermetica*10: 68–72.
Fanon, Frantz (1961) *The Wretched of the Earth*. Translated by Richard Philcox. New York: Grove Press.
Faye, Guillaume (2010) *Archeofuturism: European Visions of the Post-catastrophic Age UK*. London: Arktos.
Faye, Guillaume (2016) *The Colonization of Europe*. London: Arktos.
Feldman, Leah (2012) "Orientalism on the threshold: Reorienting heroism in late imperial Russia. *Boundary* 2(39): 2.
Feldman, Leah (2023) Trad rights: Making Eurasian whiteness at the "end of history." *Boundary* 2(50): 1.
Fenghi, Fabrizio (2020) *It Will Be Fun and Terrifying: Nationalism and Protest in Post- Soviet Russia*. Madison: University of Wisconsin Press.
Fennema, Meindert (2004) Populist parties of the Right. ASSR Working Paper 04/01 (February). Amsterdam: Amsterdam School for Social Science Research.
Ferreira, H. Helisangela Maria Andrade (2016). As plinianas de Pernambuco: O cotidiano das mulheres na Ação Integralista Brasileira(1932–1938) [Master thesis, Universidade Federal Rural de Pernambuco].
Finchelstein, Federico (2019) *From Fascism to Populism in History*. Berkeley: California University Press.
Finchelstein, Federico (2022) A Brief History of Fascist Lies. Berkeley: California University Press.
François, Stéphane (2014) The Nouvelle Droite and "tradition." *Journal for the Study of Radicalism* 8(1) (Spring): 87–106.
Freeden, Michael (1996) *Ideologies and Political Theory*. Oxford: Clarendon.
Gat, Azar (1997) Futurism, proto-Fascist Italian culture and the sources of Douhetism. War & Society 15(1):31–51.
Goldstein Alyosha, and Simón Ventura Trujillo (2021) Fascism now? Inquiries for an expanded frame. *Critical Ethnic Studies* 7(1) (Spring): 1–20.
Göpffarth, Julian (2020) Rethinking the German nation as German *Dasein*: Intellectuals and Heidegger's philosophy in contemporary German New Right nationalism. *Journal of Political Ideologies* 25(3): 248–273.
Gregor, James (2000) *The Faces of Janus: Marxism and Fascism in the Twentieth Century.New Haven*, CT:Yale University Press.
Gregor, James (2005) *Mussolini's Intellectuals: Fascist Social and Political Thought*. Princeton, NJ: Princeton University Press.

Gregor, James (2006) *The Search for Neofascism: The Use and Abuse of Social Science*. Cambridge: Cambridge University Press.

Griffin, Roger, ed. (1995) *Fascism. Oxford Readers*. Oxford: Oxford University Press.

Griffin, Roger (2000). Interregnum or endgame? The radical right in the "post-fascist" era. *Journal of Political Ideologies* 5(2): 163–178.

Griffini, Marianna (2023) *The Politics of Memory in the Italian Populist Radical Right: From Mare Nostrum to Mare Vostrum*. Routledge.

Grossmann, Matt, and David Hopkins (2015) Ideological Republicans and group interest Democrats: The asymmetry of American party politic. *Perspective on Politics* 13(1) (March): 119–139.

Guénon, René (1967) 1975 À propos de conversions. In Daniel Boulognon, ed., *Initiation et Réalisation Spirituelle*. Paris: Éditions Traditionelles, pp. 84–88.

Harrison, Olivia (2022) France a settler post-colony? MER issue 302 "Settler Colonialism's Enduring Entanglements" 04.20.

Hauwaert, Steven M. Van, Christian H. Schimpf and Régis Dandoy (2019) Populist demand, economic development and regional identity across nine European countries: Exploring regional patterns of variance *European Societies* 21(2): 303–332.

Heer, Jet (2016) The pro-Trump intellectuals who want to overthrow America. *The New Republic*, October 4.

Heidegger, Martin (2009) *Logic as the Question Concerning the Essence of Language*. Albany: State University of New York Press.

Heidegger, Martin (2014) *Introduction to Metaphysics* (2nd edition). Translated by Gregory Fried and Richard Poll. New Haven, CT: Yale University Press.

Herf, Jeffrey (1986) *Reactionary Modernism: Technology, Culture, and Politics in Weimar and the Third Reich*. Cambridge: Cambridge University Press.

Hirschman, Albert (1991) *The Rhetoric of Reaction: Perversity, Futility, Jeopardy*. Cambridge, MA: Belknap Press of Harvard University Press.

Homans, Charles (2024) Donald Trump has never sounded like this. *New York Times*, April 27.

Hull, George (2022) Epistemic ethnonationalism: Identity policing in neo-Traditionalism and decoloniality theory. *Acta Academica* 54(3): 131–155.

Hussne, Arthur (2020) Olavismo e bolsonarismo. *Revista Rosa* s/n. sur. http://revistarosa.com/1/olavismo-e-bolsonarismo.

Iamamoto, Sue A. S., Maíra Kubík Mano and Renata Summa (2023) Brazilian far-right neoliberal nationalism: Family, anti-communism and the myth of racial democracy. *Globalizations* 20(5): 782–798.

Inglehart, Ronald (1971) The silent revolution in Europe. *American Political Science Review* 65(4): 991–1017.

Inglehart, Ronald, and Pippa Norris (2017) Trump and the populist authoritarian parties: The silent revolution in reverse. *Perspectives on Politics* 15(2): 443–454.

Inglehart, Ronald, and Christian Welzel (2005) *Modernization, Cultural Change, and Democracy: The Human Development Sequence.* Cambridge: Cambridge University Press.

Jabri, Vivienne (2013) *The Postcolonial Subject Claiming Politics/Governing Others in Late Modernity.* London: Routledge.

Kallis, Aristotle (2021) The transnational co-production of interwar "fascism": On the dynamics of ideational mobility and localization. *European History Quarterly* 51(2): 189–213.

Kaltwasser, Cristoval Rovira (2012) The ambivalence of populism: Threat and corrective for democracy. *Democratization* 19(2): 184–208.

Katznelson, Ira (2003) *Desolation and Enlightenment. New York:* Columbia University Press.

Kymlicka, Will (1995) *Multicultural Citizenship: A Liberal Theory of Minority Rights.* Oxford: Oxford University Press.

Laclau, Ernesto (2005) *On Populist Reason.* London: Verso Books.

Laurelle, Marlène (2007) Alexandre Dugin: A "Eurasianist" view on Chechnya and the North Caucasus. *North Caucasus Weekly* 8(6). https://jamestown.org/program/alexandre-dugin-a-eurasianist-view-on-chechnya-and-the-north-caucasus-2.

Laurelle, Marlène (2008) *Russian Eurasianism: An Ideology of Empire.* Translated by Mischa Gabowitsch. Baltimore, MD: Johns Hopkins University Press.

Layton, Susan (1994) *Russian Literature and Empire: Conquest of the Caucasus from Pushkin to Tolstoy.* Cambridge: Cambridge University Press.

Levitsky, Steven, and David Ziblat (2018) *How Democracies Die.* New York: Penguin.

Lieberman, Robert (2002) Ideas, Institution and Political Order. *American Political Science Review* 96(4) (December): 697–712.

Lilla, Mark (2018). Two roads for the new French right. *New York Review of Books*, December 20.

Lind, Jennifer, and William Wolforth (2019) The future of the liberal order is conservative: A strategy to save the system. *Foreign Affairs* 98(2): 70–82.

Love, Jeff, and Michael Meng (2017) Heidegger and post-colonial fascism. *Nationalities Papers* 45(2): 307–320.

Lugones, María (2007) Heterosexualism and the colonial/modern gender system. *Hypatia* 22(1): 186–209.

Macnulty, Tim (2022) We take no lessons from Macron. *The Express*, September 29.

Main, Thomas (2018) *The Rise of the Alt Right*. Cambridge, MA: Bookings Institute Press.

Mammone, Andrea (2008) The transnational reaction to 1968: Neo-fascist fronts and political cultures in France and Italy. *Contemporary European History* 17(2): 213–236.

Mammone, Andrea (2009) The eternal return? Faux populism and contemporarization of neo-fascism across Britain, France and Italy. Journal of Contemporary European Studies 17(2): 171–192.

Mann, Michael (2004) *Fascists*. Cambridge: Cambridge University Press.

Mathyl, Markus (2004). The National Bolshevik Party and Arctogaia. In Roger Griffin and Matthew Feldman, eds., *Fascism: Critical Concepts in Political Science, vol. 5. Post War Fascism*. London: Routledge, pp. 185–201.

Miglio, Gianfranco (1991–1992) Towards a federal Italy. *Telos* 1991(90): 19–42.

Mignolo, Walter (2000) The geopolitics of knowledge and the colonial difference. *South Atlantic Quarterly* 101(1): 57–96.

Miller, David (1989) *Market State and Community: Theoretical Foundations of Market Socialism*. Oxford: Oxford University Press.

Millerman, Michael (2015) Russia has renewed its propaganda war by attacking liberal democratic values. *National Post*, September 3.

Moffit, Benjamin (2016) *The Global Rise of Populism: Performance, Political Style and Representation*. Stanford, CA: Stanford University Press.

Mohler, Armin (1972) *Die konservative Revolution in Deutschland 1918–1932*. Darmstadt: Wissenschaftliche Buchgesellschaft.

Morgan, John (2017) *Alt right versus New Right*. San Francisco, CA: Counter Current. www.counter-currents.com/2017/02/alt-right-versus-new-right.

Motadel, David (2014) *Islam and Nazi Germany's War*. Cambridge, MA: Harvard University Press.

Motadel, David (2019) The global authoritarian moment and the revolt against empire. *American Historical Review* 124(3): 843–877.

Mounk, Yaschka (2018) *The People against Democracy*. Cambridge, MA: Harvard University Press.

Mudde, Cas (2004) The populist zeitgeist. *Government and Opposition* 39(3): 541–563.

Müller, Jan Werner (2011) *Contesting Democracy: Political Ideas in 20th Century Europe. New Haven, CT:* Yale University Press.

Müller, Jan Werner (2016) *What Is Populism?* Philadelphia: Pennsylvania University Press.

Mutti, Claudio (2007) Islam in the eyes of Julius Evola. February 11. www.claudiomutti.com/index.php?url=6&imag=1&id_news=130.

Nagel, Angela (2018) *Kill All the Normies: Online Culture Wars from 4chan and Tumblr to Trump and the Alt-right*. Winchester: Zero Books.

Neuberger, Benyamin (1996) Black nationalism, Jews, and Zionism. *Avar Veatid* (April): 18–22.

Nolte, Ernst (1966) *Three Faces of Fascism: Action Francaise, Italian Fascism, National Socialism.* Translated by Leila Vennewitz. New York: Holt, Rhinehart and Winston.

La Nouvelle Droite de l'an 2000. *Éléments* 94 (February).

Oakeshott, Michael (1962) *Rationalism in Politics and Other Essays*. New York: Basic Books.

Oakeshott, Michael (1991) On being conservative. In *Rationalism in Politics and Other Essays* (2nd edition). Indianapolis, IN: Liberty Fund, pp. 407–437.

Orellana Pablo de, and Nicholas Michelsen (2019) Reactionary internationalism: The philosophy of the New Right. *Review of International Studies* 45(5). Special Issue on Populism (December): 748–767.

Parland, Thomas (2005) *The Extreme Nationalist Threat in Russia: The Growing Influence of Western Rightist Ideas*. Routledge.

Paxton, Robert (2005) *The Anatomy of Fascism*. New York: Vintage Books.

Payne, Stanley (1996) *A History of Fascism, 1914–1945*. Madison: Wisconsin University Press.

Pereira Goncalves, Leandro (2014) The Integralism of Plínio Salgado: Luso-Brazilian Relations. *Portuguese Studies* 30(1): 67–93.

Pfister, Rene (2019) Will Merkel be followed by darkness? *Der Spiegel*, May 28.

Piccone, Paul (1991) The crisis of liberalism and the emergence of federal populism. *Telos* 89: 7–45.

Pinheiro Ramos, Alexander (2014) O Integralismo, de Hélgio Trindade, quarenta anos depois: Uma crítica à sua recepção. *Antiteses* 7(14).

Pogge, James (2025) How long can the alliance between tech titans and the MATA faithful last? *New York Times*, January 18.

Polgreen, Lydia (2024) Restoring the past won't liberate Palestine. *New York Times*, February 18.

Quijano, Anibal (2007) Coloniality and modernity/rationality. *Cultural Studies* 21(2): 168–178.

Rabinowitz, Beth (2023) *Defensive Nationalism: Explaining the Rise of Populism and Fascism in the 21st Century.* Oxford: Oxford University Press.

Reich, Robert (2022) Putin and Trump convinced me: I was wrong about the 21 century. *The Guardian*, March 13.

Rennie, David (2022) China wants to change, or break, a world order set by others. *The Economist*. Special report, October 10.

Risse, Thomas, and Jan K. Grabowski (2008) European identity formation in the public sphere and in foreign policy. *RECON*. Online Working Paper 2008/04, pp. 9–11. www.reconproject.eu.

Rogatchevski, Andrei (2007) The National Bolshevik Party (1993–2001): A brief timeline. *New Zealand Slavonic Journal* 41: 90–112.

Rose, Matthew (2021) *A World after Liberalism*. New Haven, CT: Yale University Press.

Rosler, Andres (2023) Sionismo o Revolución: Carl Schmitt y los Judíos Alemanes. *Blog Disidencia*. October 27.

Rueda, Daniel (2020) National populism, right and left: The social-national synthesis today. *disClosure: A Journal of Social Theory* 29: 48–63.

Rydgren, Jens (2007) The sociology of the radical right. *Annual Review of Sociology* 33: 241–262.

Said, Edward (1995) *Orientalism: Western Conceptions of the Orient*. London: Penguin.

Sartre, Jean P. (2001) *Preface of Léopold Sédar Senghor. In Jean P. Sartre, Anthologie de la nouvelle poésie nègre et malgache de langue française*. Paris: Presses Universitaires de France, 1948, rééd. Quadrige, pp. ix–xliv.

Sedgwick, Mark (2016) René Guénon and Traditionalism. In Glenn Alexander Magee, ed., *The Cambridge Handbook of Western Mysticism and Esotericism*. Cambridge: Cambridge University Press, pp. 308–321.

Sedgwick, Mark, ed. (2019)*Key Thinkers of the Radical Right*. Oxford: Oxford University Press.

Sedgwick, Mark (2021) Traditionalism in Brazil: Sufism, Ta'i Chi, and Olavo de Carvalho. *Journal for the Study of Western Esotericism* 21: 159–184.

Sedgwick, Mark (2022) The localization of esotericism: Guénonian traditionalism in South America. *Nova Religio* 61(1): 35–58.

Segré, Claudio (1979) Beggar's empire: Ideology and the colonialist movement in liberal Italy. *Proceedings of the Meeting of the French Colonial Historical Society* 4: 174–183.

Sharpe, Matthew (2017) Alexander Dugin, Eurasianism, and the American election. *The Conversation*. https://theconversation.com/alexander-dugin-eurasianism-and-the-american-election-87367.

Sheehan, Thomas (1981) Myth and violence: The fascism of Julius Evola and Alain de Benoist. *Social Research* 48(1): 45–73.

Shekhovtsov, Anton (2009) Alexander Dugin and neo Eurasianism: The new right a la Russe. *Religion Compass* 3: 697–716.

Shekhovtsov, Anton (2015) Alexander Dugin and the West European New Right, 1989–1994. In Marlene *Laurelle, ed., Eurasianism and the European Far*

Right. Reshaping the Europe–Russia Relationship. Lanham, MD: Lexington Books.

Shekhovtsov, Anton, and Andrea Umland (2009) Is Aleksandr Dugin a Traditionalist? "Neo-Eurasianism" and perennial philosophy. *The Russian Review* 68 (October): 662–678.

Smith, Rogers (2001) Citizenship and the politics of people-building. *Citizenship Studies* 5(1): 73–96.

Smith, Rogers, and Desmond King (2021) White protectionism in America. *Perspectives on Politics* 19(2) (June): 460–478.

Smith, Terry (2020) *Whitelash Unmasking: White Grievances in the Ballot Box*. Cambridge: Cambridge University Press.

Snyder, Timothy (2018) *The Road to Unfreedom*. New York: Tim Duggan Books.

Snyder, Timothy (2022a) Europe's last chance for renewal. *Foreign Policy*, March 9.

Snyder, Timothy (2022b) We should say it: Russia is fascist. *New York Times*, May 19.

Spektorowski, Alberto (2012) The French New Right: Multiculturalism of the right and the recognition exclusion syndrome. *Journal of Global Ethics* 8(1): 41–61.

Spektorowski, Alberto (2023) Identity politics and the decolonization of the Western mind: The intellectual resilience of Alain de Benoist and the Nouvelle Droite. *Comparative Political Theory* 3: 97–127.

Spektorowski, Alberto (2024) Anti-Semitism, Islamophobia and anti-Zionism: Discrimination and Political Construction. *Religions* 15(74): 1–19.

Spivak, Gayatri Chakravorty (1988) Can the subaltern speak? In Cary Nelson and Lawrence Grossberg, eds., *Marxism and the Interpretation of Culture*. Chicago: University of Illinois Press, pp. 66–111.

Stanley, Jason (2018) *How Fascism Works: The Politics of Us and Them*. New York: Random House.

Sternhell, Zeev (1995) *Neither Right nor Left: Fascist Ideology in France*. Princeton, NJ: Princeton University Press.

Sternhell, Zeev (2008) How to think about fascism and its ideology. *Constellations* 15(3): 280–290.

Sternhell, Zeev, Mario Sznajder and Maia Ashéri (1994) *The Birth of Fascist Ideology: From Cultural Rebellion to Political Revolution*. Princeton, NJ: Princeton University Press.

Taggart, Paul (2004) Populism and representative politics in contemporary Europe. *Journal of Political Ideologies* 9(3): 269–288.

Taguieff, Pierre (1988) *La force du prejuge: Essai sur le racismesest doublés*. Paris: La Decouverte.

Taguieff, Pierre (1994) From race to culture: The new right's view on European Identity.*Telos* 98–9: 99–125.

Tamkin, Emily (2022) How the American Right stopped worrying and learned to love Russia. *New York Times*, February 27.

Taylor, Jared (2015) An open letter to cuckservatives. *American Renaissance*, July 30.

Teitelbaum, Benjamin (2020) *War for Eternity: Inside Bannon's Far-Right Circle of Global Power Brokers*. London: Allen Lane Books.

Teitelbaum, Benjamin (2021) *The Ideology behind the Far Right in Brazil and the World*. Sao Paulo: Fundacáo Fernando Henrique Cardoso.

Tillet, Pierrick (2017) Ukraine: Pour Alain de Benoist, la fin de la guerre froid en'a jamais eu lieu. *L'OBS*, January 27.

Tisdall, Simon (2024) Fascism is everywhere on the march. And it's Trump who sets the pace. *The Guardian* (January 24)

Tolz, Vera (2008) European, national, and (anti-)imperial: The formation of academic Oriental studies in late tsarist and early Soviet Russia. *Kritika: Explorations in Russian and Eurasian History* 9(1): 53–81.

Traverso, Enzo (2016) The End of Jewish Modernity. London: Pluto Press.

Traverso, Enzo (2019) *The New Faces of Fascism: Populism and the Far Right*. London: Verso.

Trindade, Hélgio (1979) *Integralismo: O fascismo brasileiro na década de 30*. Rio de Janeiro: DIFEL.

Umland, Andreas (2007) Post-Soviet "uncivil society" and the rise of Aleksandr Dugin: A case study of the extra parliamentary radical Right in contemporary Russia. *SSRN Electronic Journal*. https://download.ssrn.com/17/01/05/ssrn_id2892325_code1140614.pdf?response-content-disposition=inline&X-Amz-Security-Token=IQoJb3JpZ2luX2V

Urbinati, Nadia (2019) *Me the People: How Populism Transforms Democracy. Cambridge, MA:* Harvard University Press.

Valdai Discussion Group (2013) Vladimir Putin meets with members of the Valdai International Discussion Group, September 29.

Van Hauwaert, Steven, Christian Schimpf and Régis Dandoy (2019) Populist demand, economic development and regional identity across nine European countries: Exploring regional patterns of variance. European Societies 21(2): 303–325.

Varga, Mihai, and Aron Buzogány (2021) The two faces of the "global Right: *Revolutionary conservatives and national-conservatives.*Critical Sociology 4(6): 1098–1107.

Veber, Michel F. (1983) *Comentários à "Metafísica Oriental" de René Guénon*. Sao Paulo: Instituto de Estudos tradicionais.

Venner, Dominique (1993) National Bolchevisme: Des nouvelles convergences pour un front anti-systeme? *Reflex*, no. 40: 13–17.

Versluis, Arthur (2014) A conversation with Alain de Benoist. *Journal for the Study of Radicalism* 8(2) (Fall): 79–106.

Vial, Pierre (1979) *Pour une renassaince culturelle: Le GRECE prend la parole*. Paris: Copernic.

Victor, Rogério Lustosa (2005) *O integralismo nas águas do Lete: História, memória e esquecimento*. Guyana: Universidade Federal de Goiás Faculdade de Ciências Humanas e Filosofia.

Viser, Matt (2022) In fiery midterm speech, Biden says GOP's turned toward "semi-fascism." *Washington Post*, August 25.

Weyland, Kurt (2021) *Assault on Democracy: Communism, Fascism, and Authoritarianism during the Interwar Years*. Cambridge: Cambridge University Press.

Williams, Thomas (2017) The French origins of "you will not replace us." *The New Yorker*, November 27.

Wink, George (2021) *Brazil, Land of the Past: The Ideological Roots of the New Right*. Cuernavaca, Morelos, Mexico: Bibliotopia.

Wink, George (2023) Le nouvel intégrisme: Les conservateurs catholiques et la Nouvelle Droite brésilienne. *Brésil(s): Sciences humaines et sociales*, no. 23. http://journals.openedition.org/bresils/14876. https://doi.org/10.4000/bresils.14876

Winter, Brian (2018) Jair Bolsonaro's guru. *America's Quarterly*, December 17. www.americasquarterly.org/content/jair-bolsonarosguru.

Wolff, Elisabetha Cassina (2016) Evola's interpretation of fascism and moral responsibility. *Patterns of Prejudice* 50(4–5): 478–494.

Wright, Robin (2022) Does the U.S.–Russia crisis over Ukraine prove that the Cold War never ended? *The New Yorker*, February 19.

Xinhuanet (2021) www.news.cn/english/2021-12/04/c_1310351231.htm.

Yiannopoulos, Milo, and Allum Bokhari (2016) An establishment conservative's guide to the alt-right. Breitbart, March 29. www.breitbart.com/tech/2016/03/29/an-establishment-conservatives-guide-to-the-alt-right.

Young, Iris (1990) *Justice and the Politics of Difference*. Princeton, NJ: Princeton University Press.

Cambridge Elements ≡

The History and Politics of Fascism

Series Editors
Federico Finchelstein
The New School for Social Research

Federico Finchelstein is Professor of History at the New School for Social Research and Eugene Lang College in New York City. He is an expert on fascism, populism, and dictatorship. His previous books include *From Fascism to Populism in History* and *A Brief History of Fascist Lies.*

António Costa Pinto
University of Lisbon

António Costa Pinto is a Research Professor at the Institute of Social Sciences, University of Lisbon. He is a specialist in fascism, authoritarian politics, and political elites. He is the author and editor of multiple books on fascism, including (with Federico Finchelstein) *Authoritarianism and Corporatism in Europe and Latin America.*

Advisory Board
Giulia Albanese, *University of Padova*
Mabel Berezin, *Cornell University*
Maggie Clinton, *Middlebury College*
Sandra McGee Deutsch, *University of Texas, El Paso*
Aristotle Kallis, *Keele University*
Sven Reichardt, *University of Konstanz*
Angelo Ventrone, *University of Macerata*

About the Series
Cambridge Elements in the History and Politics of Fascism is a series that provides a platform for cutting-edge comparative research in the field of fascism studies. With a broad theoretical, empirical, geographic, and temporal scope, it will cover all regions of the world, and most importantly, search for new and innovative perspectives.

Cambridge Elements

The History and Politics of Fascism

Elements in the Series

Populism and Fascism
Carlos de la Torre

The Rise of Mass Parties, Liberal Italy, and the Fascist Dawn (1919–1924)
Goffredo Adinolfi

Neo-Fascism and the Far Right in Brazil
Odilon Caldeira Neto

Intellectual Post-fascism?: The Conservative Revolution, Traditionalism and the Challenge to Liberal Democracy
Alberto Spektorowski

A full series listing is available at: www.cambridge.org/CEHF

For EU product safety concerns, contact us at Calle de José Abascal, 56–1°, 28003 Madrid, Spain or eugpsr@cambridge.org.

www.ingramcontent.com/pod-product-compliance
Ingram Content Group UK Ltd.
Pitfield, Milton Keynes, MK11 3LW, UK
UKHW021828060725
460335UK00017B/179